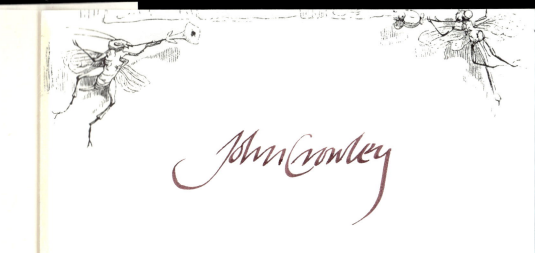

John Crowley

This special signed edition is limited to 600 numbered copies and 26 lettered copies.

This is copy 187

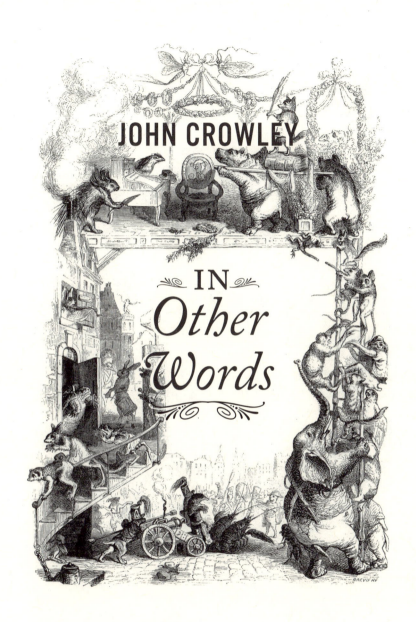

JOHN CROWLEY

IN Other Words

SUBTERRANEAN PRESS 2006

In Other Words
Copyright © 2006 by John Crowley. All rights reserved.

Dust Jacket Illustration
Copyright © 2006 by To Come. All rights reserved.

Design and layout by Alligator Tree Graphics

FIRST EDITION

ISBN
1-59606-062-X

Subterranean Press
PO Box 190106
Burton, MI 48519

www.subterraneanpress.com

CONTENTS

Foreword   1

Myself and Some Others
Reading and Writing in the Former End of the World   7
Tips and Tricks for Successful Lying   15
A Modern Instance: Magic, Imagination, and Power   25
The Labyrinth of the World and the Paradise of the Heart   37

Five Writers
Robert Louis Stevenson   55
    Robert Louis Stevenson and the Dilemma of an Uncritical Readership   55
    Robert Louis Stevenson by Frank McLynn and The Letters of Robert Louis Stevenson, Volumes III and IV, edited by Ernest Mehew   65
    Mary Reilly by Valerie Martin   70

Thomas M. Disch   74
T.H. White   87
Vladimir Nabokov   94
    The Magician's Doubts by Michael Wood, and The Stories of Vladimir Nabokov, edited by Dimitri Nabokov   94
    VN: The Life and Art of Vladimir Nabokov by Andrew Field, and The Enchanter by Vladimir Nabokov, translated by Dimitri Nabokov   97
    The Man from the U.S.S.R. and Other Plays   100

Anthony Burgess   103
    The Kingdom of the Wicked   103
    The Pianoplayers   104

Any Old Iron	107
Enderby's Dark Lady	109
Little Wilson and Big God	111

Some Others

The Arabian Nightmare by Robert Irwin	117
The Young Visiters: Or, Mr Salteena's Plan by Daisy Ashford	120
Labrador by Kathryn Davis	122
Pinto and Sons by Leslie Epstein	125
In the Beauty of the Lilies by John Updike	128
Story of O by Pauline Reage	132
Hermit in Paris by Italo Calvino, translated by Martin McLaughlin	133
Adventures of the Artificial Woman by Thomas Berger	136
Being Dead by Jim Crace	139
The Fermata by Nicholson Baker	142
The Everlasting Story of Nory by Nicholson Baker	145
The Book of Evidence by John Banville	148
Athena by John Banville	151

Some Nonfictions

The Mask of Nostradamus by James Randi	157
The Queen's Conjuror by Benjamin Woolley	160
Fragments for a History of the Human Body: Parts I, II, III, edited by Michel Feher	163
Wonders and the Order of Nature 1150-1750 by Lorraine Daston and Katherine Park	166

Comix

Ben Katchor	173
Krazy Kat: the Comic Art of George Herriman by Patrick McDonnell, Karen O'Connell and Georgia Riley de Havenon	180
Winsor McCay: His Life and Art by John Canemaker	183
Tintin in the New World by Frederic Tuten	186

The World of Edward Gorey *by Clifford Ross and Karen Wilkin*	189
Walt Kelley	192

FOREWORD

"*A* FOREWORD TO THE READER is an afterword to the author," as Anthony Burgess says in the foreword of his own autobiography, of which my review is included in what follows. "The author knows what has been written, the reader has yet to find out." The temptation to apologize, explain, underscore, pre-empt valid criticism, or head off contempt is strong, and gratitude for the reader's having picked up the volume and read even thus far mingles with an impulse to assure him or her that there is no reason whatever not to put it back down again if the least tedium develops. The greatest virtue I can claim for the present volume is that it is short, the subjects change every few pages, and many of the subjects are interesting in themselves, my treatment of them aside.

Some of the pieces that follow are seeing print for the first time. *Reading and Writing in the Former End of the World* was prepared for an appearance with two other writers before a venerable reading club sponsored by the Cleveland *Plain Dealer*. My novel *The Translator* was just appearing, and this piece attempts to describe it and its context and myself. The piece that follows was submitted for the Bechtel Prize offered by *Readers & Writers Magazine*, and was not selected; I'm glad to have found a place for it, though my writing students have heard much of its content over the years. The paper on Robert Louis Stevenson was delivered at an international clebration of the 100th anniversary of Robert Louis Stevenson hosted by the Beinecke Library at Yale, where I teach classes in fiction writing.

Several of the longer pieces included resulted from an invitation of one kind or another. For the Beinecke event I was asked to give a paper on any aspect of Stevenson that interested me. The piece on Utopia and Fiction was the result of an invitation from Clara Park at Williams College to address a colloquium in the History of

Ideas; he topic of the colloquium was "Civilization". (The invitation was made at the urging of Paul Park, who is Professor Park's son.) The essay on magic and Ioan Culianu resulted from an invitation to address the International Conference on the Fantastic in the Arts. The essays on the work of Thomas Disch and Ben Katchor resulted from invitations from the Yale Review. The same for the essay on *Pogo* and the Boston Review: What would I like to write about? the editors asked. Very pleasant to hear!

Most of the short reviews, though, are of fiction assigned to me by editors; and while I have always reserved the right to refuse a book if, after a few pages, I found it unreadable (what good would a review of a book be whose reviewer found it agony to read through? What potential reader would need that review?) I often thus read books and authors unknown to me; it was through this lottery that I came to know John Banville, whom I admire now as much as I do any living writer, and Jim Crace, whose *Being Dead* is a touchstone for me.

Reviewing fiction, as a trade, is fairly thankless. (Cyril Connolly famously called it "the White Man's Grave of journalism," which I take to mean the place where many would-be writers and critics end up and from which they may never escape with their ambitions intact—a thing possibly true in Connolly's day, with a highly literate population and dozens of journals publishing extended reviews read by relatively large readerships; now it tempts few, and pays even fewer a living.) There's eternally the chance of not recognizing genius, and the greater chance of praising the ephemeral far beyond its worth, both of which will make you look silly, and may result in timidity on the one hand when faced with something new, or in a self-justifying *saeve indignatio* and grandstanding for its own sake on the other. I've been fortunate to have had two great editors for much of my reviewing, Nina King at *Newsday* and the Washington *Post* and then Michael Dirda at the *Post*, who have both allowed me to write about more than fiction. It's often more gratifying to engage with the facts and notions in biographies, histories, books about science or art, than to try to describe and evaluate another novel. Many of those I asked to be allowed to take on. Some of these are included here, such as the book on Nostradamus by a magician, The Amazing Randi.

I have tried to arrange all these fugitive pieces in an order that will make them seem at least a little less fugitive. I have ignored their dates of composition (to arrange them in time order would have been to reveal how little I've improved at this over the years) and grouped them by—well, by groups, sort of. I was a little surprised when gathering them that I'd written so much on the comics and comics-related subjects, so those make a group. I have gathered all my reviews of Anthony Burgess and all my reviews of books by and about Vladimir Nabokov together, in an attempt to make larger pictures, and all the writing about Robert Louis Stevenson, including a review of *Mary Reilly* by Valerie Martin.

These groupings make more evident, however, a special drawback of a collection like this one. Readers who do more than dip into the volume will begin to note small repetitions of several kinds. The story is told (I forget by whom) of a young writer who was disappointed by André Gide's table talk—Gide tended to repeat a lot of the clever things he'd already said in print. What did the listener expect? Few writers' stores of anecdote and witticism are bottomless; in reviews I can usually assume that readers won't remember an observation from its earlier ephemeral appearances (I often don't myself). But now here they all are, bound together, with their own ISBN, as immortal as paper and ink may be nowadays, and with these obvious tics and all their other faults upon them. I have not attempted to correct any of these, though in some instances I have reverted to my own original version of a piece, which was edited for space or some less imperative reason by the various journals involved, and in a few instances I have corrected small matters of fact.

My thanks to Bill Sheehan for believing that this collection would be of interest to readers, and encouraging me to believe it too.

Conway, Massachusetts
May 4, 2005

MYSELF AND SOME OTHERS

READING AND WRITING IN
THE FORMER END OF THE WORLD

I'VE BEEN THINKING a lot in the last year or two about what I call the Former End of the World: that time—it coincided with my growing into adulthood—when a terrible doom hung over all of us, one that could drop on us at any moment, without warning or almost without warning. Everyone I know who grew up in those years had the experience of dreaming that the doom has actually come, the bombs have fallen: the sense of horror and wrongness coupled with a certainty that yes, of course it's happened, as it had to. We lived in those days with the bomb every day, and rarely thought about it; we had decided to act as though we were safe, while knowing we were not.

I'm thinking now about reading and writing in that age: not grownup reading and writing, about which I knew very little, just as I knew next to nothing about how grownups were grappling with the paradoxes of the bomb: but about my own life of reading and writing in the end of the world.

I can remember a time before I could read, but not a time before I liked reading. I can remember sitting with my parents, each of them with a book, and me with my book too, like theirs a thick book full of dense lines of type; I'd scan the pages, and smile or sigh or laugh a little as they did, and turn my pages when they turned theirs. It seemed to me a delightful and absorbing activity even when I wasn't actually able to do it, and became more so when I could.

When my family moved from Vermont to northeastern Kentucky, our lives changed profoundly in several ways, but in two ways distinctly: there was television, and there was no library.

The absence of a library didn't stop us from reading. My mother somehow found out that books could be obtained from the state library in Lexington, sent to you in a brown beaverboard case which you mailed back to them when you'd read the books. They sent you books you asked for or books that seemed similar, which made for some interesting reading experiences. They: I imagined a librarian like the one back in Brattleboro, Vermont, gray and smart and wonderfully fussy about books. I enjoyed describing this system in a novel of mine called *Love & Sleep*.

So I went on reading as much as ever. I don't know how I came by them, but I started reading Sherlock Holmes, and the novels of Thomas Costain, and best of all the wonderful history of archaeology *Gods, Graves and Scholars*.

It's supposed to be harder now than it was in the past to interest children of the age I was then—eleven, twelve—in reading, and even harder to get the attention of teenagers and young adults. I don't know if the demographics really bear this out—when a phenomenon like Harry Potter appears, young people seem as willing as ever to put their feet up and absorb vast quantities of print. But if it is true that they like reading less, I think the reason might lie in an unwillingness to be bored, or an intolerance for boredom that results from the vast range of splendid entertainments constantly available all around them, all of them expertly designed to fend off the slightest twinge of boredom lest they be clicked off in favor of another. Long books—books from the age when they had few or no competitors as entertainments—necessarily involve stretches of boredom, or at least somnolence or low levels of excitement. There's the boredom of old-fashioned fully featured story-telling, like Scott's or Dickens' or Dumas's, which despite the thrilling head of steam they can eventually work up, can be boring to embark on, and boring as they build a milieu for some chapters: like the long coal trains of my Kentucky town, starting to roll, car after car tugged into motion until inertia took over.

I liked that kind of boredom, actually; I liked decoding a text I didn't at first fully understand; I didn't mind stuff that went above my head for a time. I think there are many now who also like this, and I know there were many back then who didn't. There are always those who can let themselves down step by step into a long strange book, who find it natural even if they weren't raised, as I was, to regard it as a natural way to spend time and feeling. I knew two Puerto Rican sisters much later in New York who never finished high school, whose first language wasn't English, and one of them rarely read anything, but the other—well once she was baby-sitting in an upscale apartment, and from a shelf of books I'm sure were there only for decoration, she picked out an old one she'd never heard of, and she read it all the way through, touched and moved (and bored). It was *Uncle Tom's Cabin*. She told me the plot.

In the novel I've written about the days of the cold war and the threat of nuclear annihilation, those dread things aren't often talked about, and when they are talked about it's almost in shame, as though ordinary people had no right to open such subjects, or as though to talk about them might bring the disaster closer. It wasn't the only topic not talked about then; there was sex and race and poverty in America and disability and mental illness and homosexuality. It was disloyal to remember America's radical past, and a shocking breach of propriety to suggest that someone might once have belonged to a radical political organization.

Kit Malone, the main character in this book, calls it the age of not saying things. I created in Kit a character who is wholly naive about almost everything in the world, a child admittedly of a sheltering and careful family practiced in evasions, but ignorant of even what others her age knew about reality; and at the same time weirdly learned about poetry and the process of writing and reading. The character may strike readers as inauthentically extreme, and all I can say in my defense or hers is that I was a person very much like her myself.

I seem to have grown up English. My mother was a reader of English mystery stories, a quoter of tags and bits out of English poetry and the Anglican hymnal (I didn't always know which was which—"Where every prospect pleases, and only Man is vile," she used to say, looking at a landscape, and this turned out to be not a line from Pope but from an Isaac Watts hymn). My earliest books—"Pat the Bunny" aside, of which I inherited a first edition from my sister—were English, and continued to be: A.A. Milne's books of poetry, then the Alice books, then *The Wind in the Willows*, Sherlock Holmes, T.H. White. Reading *The Wind in the Willows* in bed in my room with tea and toast (I was sick, I suppose) is one of the most memorable reading experiences of my life.

Then poetry, which you could graduate to naturally out of those English books that were full of references to it. We memorized poetry in school in those days, too, and much though not all of it was English: "The Charge of the Light Brigade," and "I wandered lonely as a cloud," and "Shoot if you must this old gray head." By myself I read Omar Khayyam, which everybody of the age just before mine, to which I actually secretly seemed to belong, could recite from; and Swinburne—I may be the latest-born American teenager who memorized Swinburne—and "The Rime of the Ancient Mariner" and "Ozymandias." Nobody made me read these things and no one suggested which others might go well with them; I just read on, poking in the library and the old books on the family shelf. It helped that I didn't particularly care what other boys thought of me; or rather I found it hard to conceive that they had any opinions about me at all, though I'm sure now that they did.

The Elizabethan dramatists were my next find. I thought then—I'm a junior or senior in high school now—that what I wanted to do was to be a theatrical designer or impresario, and my taste in theater ran to the heroic and even grandiose. I loved John Webster—I was delighted to see he got a cameo in the recent film *Shakespeare in Love* as a nasty-minded boy—and others even less commonly read now, like John Ford, who had some good titles—*'Tis Pity She's a Whore*, *The Broken Heart*. I loved Tourneur, whose pseudo-Italian characters had wonderfully expressive names—I remember a bastard son named Spurioso.

All this time I was writing as well as reading. I discovered, like my character Kit Malone, that I could write in blank verse, and did so with a vengeance. I wrote plays, also sometimes in blank verse—well, I began them; and stories and a historical novel that would transmute, many years later, into my first published book, a science fiction novel by then, called *The Deep*.

In all this I've said nothing about the threat of nuclear destruction, the abyss on whose lip I claim we stood—on whose lip we *did* stand. That was the time I grew up in, the days of that end of the world. But I didn't think about it, except in dreams. I didn't write about it, I didn't read about it. On *The Twilight Zone* now and then there would be a story set in the world after the end, which induced in me either an eerie dreamlike foreboding which even now I can feel—or a jaded resistance, or a laugh. That was how we lived. Many of you remember. There were people you knew—everyone heard about them, maybe your family was among them—who had built a bomb shelter—no, check that, it was a *fallout* shelter; everyone knew bomb shelters were futile. But I lived as though I were safe, in a culture new and present to me but lying largely in the past; and it seemed that, far from coming to an end, nothing at all in my world would ever change or be different. Ike would always be President. Pius XII would always be Pope. Russia would always be Communist. The world would always be divided in two.

I know now that my feelings were those of an adolescent who was yet to discover that the world changes, and more—that it will change because he, and his generation, challenges it. The world I grew up in was going to undergo terrible and thrilling changes and all that frozen divided nay-saying would fall away like the outward crusts of monsters in horror movies to reveal an unsuspected other being hidden within, a power who had been there all along.

Now, my coming of age really did correspond to an upheaval in the world at large, everybody experienced it or noticed it, from Beijing to Paris to San Francisco. But I believe that everyone growing up must undergo a revolution like that, must see the world break open and show new possibilities never suspected before, the Old Age get up on its stone legs and step down off its pedestal and start to dervish—I'm sure it happened in the 1930s for radically inclined youth (and youth is radical, or ought to be) and I'm sure that it happened, too, to young people who had just come through the War and were exercising their strengths and grappling with possibilities and daring the powers right then in the 1950s when I was home learning to write blank verse and figuring how to avoid going to Mass. I know it's so. Gore Vidal for one talks about it. I don't intend to present my experience as universal. It was only universal in that it filled up all the world I knew. But there's more than one history of the world; one for each of us, probably.

In any case it was during that sudden and wonderful upheaval of the world, when everybody started talking about all the things that we couldn't talk about, not excepting sex and world peace and radical change and the magic possibilities of existence and the wickedness of our leaders and the danger the earth was in—well you know, they haven't shut up since—that I began seriously to write fiction. I had for some years tried to get away from writing—trying to escape my fate, maybe—and get into movies instead, and had worked as a photographer and a commercial artist. And when I did return to fiction it wasn't to any part of that tradition I'd grown up within at all. I wrote a long strange story about a distant future in which there is no social organization, no government, no family, and—no reading and writing. The book was called (by me) *Learning to Live with it*. No one wanted to publish it. It appeared long afterward under another title: *Engine Summer*.

Writing and finishing that first draft, though, was one of the absolutely most gratifying experiences of my life, a *physical* pleasure up there with the one or two best that might automatically spring to mind, and I bent my mind to repeating it. I decided that, having finished a novel, the next thing I would do was write one that could be published. I took up that old historical novel and rewrote it set on a distant planet. I became a science fiction writer.

It seemed like a good career move at the time. Very many strange and wonderful books were being published as science fiction just then, and it was a great way to get a first novel published and read, if your mind or talent ran at all to the odd or offbeat. Metafiction, magic realism, philosophical romance, dream stories—they were all being published then as SF. It's far less the case now.

So since then my work has hovered in a kind of nameless one-person ghetto. A critic of science fiction said once that my early SF novels seemed as though they were written by someone who had heard about science fiction but hadn't ever read any, which was almost the case. Those early novels are now being reprinted, in a single volume called *Otherwise*, without the SF label.

Sort of the opposite happened to my next book. It returned into the tradition of English story-telling and the Victorian novel I grew up in; it had a double title—*Little, Big; or, The Fairies' Parliament*. It had epigraphs for every chapter, and marginal glosses, and it was very long, and it began "On a certain day in June, 19__, a certain young man was making his way Northward from the great City," etc. etc. And it had fairies and fairy tales and references to Alice in Wonderland and Arthur Rackham and Christopher Robin and *Bruno and Sylvie* and all that had been dear to me as a child. My publishers hoped for great things from this book. They took the fairies out of the title and presented it in a tasteful cover. And it sold a few copies; over time it became a cult book. Reprinted as a fantasy novel, though, it has reached large numbers of readers. Now it has come out again, this time no longer as fantasy but as—a book, a novel.

Twenty years passed.

(That's the kind of line the books I've loved can get away with.)

In those years I got married, became the parent of twin girls born on the 14th of February (we call them Val 'n' Tina, but not officially), became a teacher of writing at Yale, and worked on a single novel, though one that has appeared in three separate volumes so far: the novel is called *Ægypt*, and so is the first volume. It's about magic, and history, and how the world in one lifetime can turn from one thing into another thing. It's also about writing a book, and—secretly—about being a character in one.

If becoming a science fiction novelist looks like a somewhat perverse career choice now, embarking on a four-volume novel that would take a quarter-century to put before the public seems far more so. But we'll see. I seem to myself to be like one of those generals whose extreme strategies win them eternal fame if they work, and if they don't, well... Right at this moment, the first two volumes of the Ægypt series are available only as ebooks, from ElectricStroy.com; the third is out of print; and I'm writing the fourth.* When it's done, I hope that all four will return to print. It will be quite a relief.

Meanwhile there is this book, about reading and writing in the end of the world. It's about an exiled Russian poet, who comes to the United States at the height of the Cold War, just before the Cuban missile crisis. He's provided with a teaching job at a Midwestern university a lot like the one I went to, and there he meets the young woman, Kit, whose growing up resembles my own. And they form a friendship, a love even, that turns on the writing life: on poetry and the possibility of saying what can't be said. I tried to create in it a true picture of the world as it appeared to someone like Kit Malone then, and to place it in the history around

---

*The last volume has since been completed and will be published in 2007. [Author's note]

it; I tried to bring to it the flavor of Russian literature and Russian poetry and the Russian predicament then. And there is the bomb that hovers always over it.

But above all and at bottom it's a romance: in the sense that it's a kind of fable or fairy tale, and in the sense that it's a love story. Maybe some reader will say of it that it seems to be a love story written by someone who hasn't read many love stories, and that may be so, but may not be a drawback. The inspirations for the book were many, but the one I remember most vividly was listening to my daughters performing the love song from *Titanic*, one playing the piano, one singing about a love beyond death. And I thought, yes: like that.

The Former End of the World is more remote now, I suppose, for which we can only feel grateful. But now once again, and wholly unexpectedly, we feel threatened, as a nation and as individuals, in our own land and our own homes, by a menace foreign and far away and obscure to us, and at the same time among us, unknown. A kind of solemn unchallengeable patriotism is going around again. The government is again assumed to know what ordinary citizens don't, and trusted to make awesome decisions we can't question. It's not a new End of the World, but it might be a new age of not saying things. I wonder what kind of dreams it will issue in for those growing up now—and what kinds of books they'll write.

2002

TIPS AND TRICKS
FOR SUCCESSFUL LYING

When I was a junior in college, a very long time ago, I received a Ford Foundation three-year scholarship—recipients were given money for junior and senior years, a summer study grant, and a sum for a first year of graduate school. Graduate study was a rarer thing to take up then, and the Ford Foundation wanted to give a push to people willing to consider being teachers. One requirement of the scholarship was a special course in the philosophy of education—a very pleasant seminar, taught by a fine teacher, who solicited our thoughts on how we would approach the problems of innovative teaching in our own field. My "field", insofar as I actually had one, was English, with a specialty in creative writing, so in the seminar I devoted myself to thinking of innovative ways of teaching writing, by which I meant fiction, the only kind that captured my own imagination.

In fact, though I was very pleased to have won the Ford Foundation's approval, and its money, I had very little intention of teaching anything to anybody—the idea seemed strange to me, and I doubted I would ever be good at it. My speculations as to how writing might be taught innovatively were pretty unrelated to how the actual work of education was getting done. I started by thinking about the New Math, which was just then at the height of its popularity. One of the features of New Math, which alarmed parents (and probably delighted kids) was that basic arithmetic wasn't taught first—concepts were taught first, number theory, set theory and so on—and arithmetic only after that. How could this model apply to writing? Well, I thought, a New Language course would not teach reading and writing first—those were mechanical skills that could come later. What kids need first is an understanding of story, story-telling, and narrative. How about starting with a course in Lying? A teacher would assign a problem—let's say you didn't do your math homework; now come up with a good story of why. This would not only give students practice in the number theory of fiction, so to speak, but insight into why stories get told—because we need them, for lots of reasons, to make things better, or at least to make sense of life.

I never got a chance to apply my New Language concepts, probably fortunately—I never even started graduate school, disappointing the Foundation. I went to work. I made a living in images first, as a photographer, and then in words, doing every kind of jobbery that offered itself, writing advertising, public relations, catalogue copy, documentary films. I began at last to write fiction of my own, and have continued in it to this day.

Some ten years ago, however, I was given an opportunity to teach a class in the writing of fiction, and that class turned into two, and now I have been teaching what at most schools (though not at Yale, my university) is called Creative Writing for so long that I consider myself a teacher after all. Except for the writing of my own fiction, I have found teaching writing and working with student writers the most gratifying and rewarding work I've ever done.

It is fashionable now to disparage the teaching of creative writing as an impossibility—how can creativity be taught? How (beyond offering encouragement on the one hand and sharp editing on the other) could the teacher of creative writing actually teach anything at all? Creativity belongs to the student—it can't be infused or imparted by teaching—and the power to make something of a potential resides as much within the student as the potential itself does. The paradoxical nature of teaching creative writing is sharpest when grades are to be assigned. It seems as odd to grade students on the quality of the work their talent has generated as to grade them on their looks, or their height. On the other hand, to rank work in creative writing not by its real worth as original creation but by how hard a student worked and how much effort was put forth seems to reward things not essential to the value of a work of art. It is this paradox that for many years kept Yale from offering many courses in creative writing; there is still no real major in creative writing at Yale, and no MFA program at the graduate level.

Given what seems to be the essential impossibility of doing what they claim to be doing, creative writing teachers (those who don't hold the process in amused contempt, and themselves as well for engaging in it) talk much about unlocking their students' resources, opening their eyes to the world they must engage with, and guiding them to be the best writers they can be. There is no doubt that these things occur in the interactions between committed students and fine teachers, and can be the unforgettable first step for a writer—but it's difficult to imagine how the ability to do these things might be fostered in teachers. We return to the mystery of the individual gift. I am also intensely aware (I need only examine the evaluations of my classes that my students file) that a teacher who is inspiring to one student can be a bore and an obstacle to another.

One unique body of knowledge that writers bring to the courses they teach is their own experience of the creative process, its possibilities and pitfalls—but the experience of one writer isn't that of another. I recently attended a reading by a fine writer and fellow teacher of mine at Yale. When she was done, there were questions from students, and one asked how she knew, at the beginning, where her story would eventually go. She didn't, she said—that's not how writing is done—as she always tells her students, writers begin with persons, and let them carry the story where they will, the writer discovering it along with them. Listening, I felt a certain concern for the students we have both taught, since I would in fact never say such a thing, and I believe my characters are bound to do just as I tell them, and complete the pattern I have already determined, while *seeming* to act from free will. How are students to learn from such contrary, and closely-held, certainties?

There are of course the great works of the past to study, and derive principles for practice from. Most courses in writing will take up Chekhov's *Lady with the Dog* or Raymond Carver's *Cathedral* or Faulkner's *Rose for Emily* or something more to the teacher's individual taste, and attempt to determine what in it is valuable, how it is made, what causes the effect it has on reader. "What is this guy trying to say?" they ask, as though he or she could only say simple things—love is hard, we must have compassion for one another, acts have unintended consequences—in elaborate parables. One of the standard methods of learning painting is (or formerly was) to copy other paintings—sit down before a Leonardo or a Parmigianino and see how close you could come to reproducing it. Unfortunately the method, though it may work in several arts, doesn't work in writing—it is central to the greatness of a great work of fiction that its methods and its successes are entirely its own, its effects and the particular means by which they are achieved are actually one thing, and inextricable. It may be more illuminating to study lesser works, whose means belong to everybody to use, to make more of the same.

Is there then no real body of craft knowledge that a teacher can impart to all students, which all aspiring writers can make use of? The many common rules that beginning writers commit to memory admit of as many exceptions as proofs when actual writing is considered. *Show, don't tell*, says the writing teacher, sure that her own practice and the work of admired writers illustrate this truth; but, as the great critic Wayne Booth points out in *The Rhetoric of Fiction*, all fiction is actually nothing but telling—what else can it be when the medium is words?—and if the desired goal is intensity, immediacy, involvement and lifelikeness, the great Tellers like George Eliot and Dickens are certainly as full of these things as the Showers like Hemingway and Raymond Carver. We all know it, but to admit it kills the rule, and we are left with nothing to say.

Or are we? Can there be a way of describing prose fiction that is at once generally applicable and also useful to writers? I think there can be.

David Lodge is both a novelist and a teacher of literature (or was, before his writing career flourished sufficiently to allow him to quit his day job). He was among those who found the strategies and inquiries of what is called Theory—that system of literary analysis derived from post-structuralist sociology, late Marxism and psychoanalytic thought, and the inquiries of such thinkers as Jacques Derrida and Roland Barthes—could be of great practical use to the working writer, however destructive they might be when wielded in the hands of critics. His books *The Modes of Modern Writing* and *After Bakhtin* showed me how some (though by no means all) of the concepts employed in Theory could be useful in the practical work of teaching writing and understanding my own practice.

The concepts of structuralism, and the more corrosive ones of post-structuralism, had great advantages over earlier critical theory as regards prose fiction. In these systems, the intentions of the writer, the expressive realism of the fictional manner and the moral force granted by the writer to his material, the accuracy of his or her description of the world (*mimesis*)—all of which were pretty subjective and soft as critical *schema*—were not only not to be considered, they were actually said to form no part of the work of fiction, except as a temporary illusion created by the reader in the act of reading. Fictions were groups of signifiers and narrative units whose meaning did not precede the reading of the work (or *text*, the term preferred as being less value-laden), and were ungoverned by the writer's intentions. In fact, the French post-structural thinkers, with characteristically literal logical thoroughness, determined that there was no author at all, and if there was a text at all, it was entirely ambiguous, unfixed in meaning.

David Lodge saw the power of working with structuralism (the title of one of his critical books), and turning from the subjective consideration of the unique value and power of individual achievement to the study of codes, conventions and rules that govern all story-telling, indeed all communication whatever. Structuralist analysis refused to "privilege" the canonical text over the folktale or the TV commercial or even the fashion show. It disposed of the long-standing "intentional fallacy"—the idea that the writer has a particular conception in her mind, a vision of life or a message, which she wraps up in a fictional story about imagined people, and leaves lying around for others, unknown to her, to find, unwrap the wrappings of story, and receive the message. Thus were torn down (or "deconstructed") the two poles of older criticism, which so frustrated the formulation of useful rules for effective fiction: the idea of the unique nature of any acheived fictional enterprise, and the idea that fiction is a (rather clumsy) way of passing a thought or vision from one mind to another ("what is this guy trying to say?").

On the other hand, as Lodge says, no working writer is going to accept "the death of the author," as Barthes called it in a famous essay written back in revolutionary 1968. Authors know that in fact they do precede the fictions they write; that they have suffered and labored in the creation of them; that their goal *is* a kind of analysis of, or thought about, or vision of, a part of our shared life, and not merely a clutch of abstract signifiers. Even as the writer experiences his creation as not entirely his own, and the voices he transcribes onto the page as not all forged by himself, he also knows that *intention* and *agency* are central to the process.

The thinker who provided a way out of this impasse and showed a positive way ahead to Lodge (and through Lodge, to myself, and through me—at least a little, I hope and believe—to my students) had actually nearly completed his life's work when the Theory boom began; his name was Mikhail Bakhtin, and the reason his contribution took so long to be noticed was that he had written in Stalin's Soviet Union, prevented from publishing or travel, and living under a nearly lifelong cloud.

Bakhtin's central contribution to the theory of language was his conviction that a word or a statement is not only a *sign* but an *act*. "The word in living conversation is directly, blatantly, oriented towards a future answer word... It provokes an answer, anticipates it and structures itself in the answer's direction." Bakhtin's view was that while the traditional canonical modes of writing—epic, tragedy, lyric poetry—were *monologic*, expressive of a single point of view and vision of the world described, fiction and the novel are inherently *dialogic*, not only in that they include dialogue, i.e., the voices of characters speaking in their own right, but because the whole text includes, echoes, reproduces, parodies and alludes to a whole range of social and literary voices, deploying devices, clichés, turns of phrase and tropes *in expectation* of an (ungovernable, but manipulable) reader's response. The act of writing fiction is an act of speaking in voices, structured in expectation of a response. The voices are as present in the *telling* as much as in the *showing*.

Some of this dialogic inclusiveness of fiction is automatic, as it is in conversation, but in writing it is, at least to a point, under the writer's control, and available to him or her as a tool. "The possibility of employing on the plane of a single work discourses of various types, with all their expressive capacities intact, without reducing them to a common denominator—this is one of the most characteristic features of prose," says Bakhtin—and the *conscious* manipulation of this polyphony is the great achievement of modern prose fiction from Dickens and Dostoevsky down to the present.

What does recognition of the principle mean for a writer's work? How do you *get better* at this conscious manipulation? Much of my work with students is directed toward helping them to see what a complex thing is this relation between writer's resources and reader's response. Seymour Chatman, working in the theory of "reader response" following Bakhtin and Russian formalism, makes the following schematic rendering of the basic relationships:

Real author → [Implied author → Narrator(s) →
Narratee(s) → Implied reader →] Real reader

Two of these persons are living humans (though not necessarily living at the same time), and they are the *real author* (myself, e.g., in my physical person) and the *real reader* (an actual other human). All the other persons, the ones between the brackets, exist inside the book. Thus, the *implied author*: Even in a novel or story written in the first person, or one in which the narration is restricted to the narrowest range of reportage (like the French *nouveau roman* of thirty years ago) there is an author speaking. We do not think that we are experiencing Huck Finn directly; we know that we are listening inwardly to a story told by an author, Mark Twain, who is constructing the events, shaping our view of them, and speaking to us about life and the passage of time. (That this author, the implied author, is a different being from the actual historical author, is shown by the fact that we always refer to the implied author in the present tense: "Here Dickens is saying... Dickens builds the suspense... Dickens's skill is remarkable...", etc. The historical person we describe in the past tense.)

The reason that a book written by a computer or the books written by chance in the Library of Babel conceived by Jorge Luis Borges would be of no interest to us beyond their oddity is that they are *directed at no one*. The *implied reader* is the person that the all the polyphonic voices of author, narrator(s) and narratee(s) are addressing, whose response the author is eliciting—not just a general response to the book as a whole, as though to a sunset or a good dinner, but a page-by-page, sentence-by-sentence response from a consciousness that is in effect created by the author's utterance: the reply that his utterance posits.

Can you see (I ask my students) what a huge opportunity is opened to you in the complexities of the relations between readers and writers? This is to me the central mystery of writing: I know that every sentence I write is directed at somebody, even maybe the "he said"s. I know that my challenge is to engage that somebody, to listen to that somebody's responses, to anticipate those responses, and act accordingly. As I engage with this reader, I can Lead Her Down the Garden Path, I can Play Fair, I can Pull the Rug Out, I can Bob and Weave, I can Speak Frankly, or do any of these things in the guise of doing any of the others. I can do it in "my own" voice, a la Thackeray, addressing the "dear reader"; or in a voice *like* my own, but a voice that is allowed to make any kind of judgment or insight, as Pynchon's narrating voice does; or through another screening narrative voice or voices (through which I'll still be sought—and found); or in a closed-mouthed, neutral, just-the-facts voice that defeats readers' queries even as it invites them. (In my second book, *Beasts*, I constructed—not quite consciously—an omniscient narrator voice that, while it never made any remarks on its own account, was recognizably that of a certain kind of person: a woodsman, a serious-minded, earth-bound, practical guy—the right author for that book—though he certainly wasn't me.)

The important thing (I tell them, those students) is that *these things are up to you*. They are choices you make, and if you make them unconsciously in creative rapture, you will have to assess them when sober again, and see what you said, *as* whom, *to* whom.

The opportunities implicit in becoming aware of the complex relations of writer and reader aren't the only strategy I learned from Theory. My toolbox is full of things I have drawn from the Russian formalist critics, the narratologists and reader-response theorists like Chatman, and others who have come, as David Lodge puts it in the title of a book, "after Bakhtin". I am behindhand in all these studies, but I have no ambition to be a cutting-edge critic—I am only gathering useful tools for my (and my students') toolbox.

The Russian formalists around Bakhtin, for instance, made a useful distinction. It works like this: Suppose that every story is a description of events that took or could take place in the real world outside books. Suppose, they said, you could extract this story from the book and regard it as a set of events that have actually taken place. They called this artifact, which of course can't really exist, the *fabula*. The actual written story, as a treatment of the fabula, they called the *sjuzet*. (If you don't like these odd terms, you could call them Story and Discourse, or Tale and Treatment.) By comparing the two, we begin to see certain interesting features of the actual written story as compared with the imaginary real-world story:

In the fabula—the story as it would take place in the world—every personage has an equal and full consciousness of the events from their own viewpoint. In the sjuzet, however, only certain persons have consciousness of the events; certain viewpoints matter more than others.

In the fabula, things only happen once. In the sjuzet, they can happen more than once, recounted from differing points of view.

Time in the fabula differs in several ways from time in the sjuzet: In the fabula, every minute takes exactly one minute to pass, every hour takes exactly one hour. In the sjuzet, some hours take longer than other hours; some years take less time than some minutes. "Twenty-five years now passed," the narrator tells us; and then proceeds to chronicle the waking and rising and breakfasting of a character on a particular day for many pages.

In the fabula, time always moves from the present into the future, leaving the past behind.

In the sjuzet, a story can move from the present to the past: events can unfold in reverse order to the fabula. Time can move in two directions at once: a character's story can advance in time even as his life is recounted in reverse, from old age toward youth.

How time passes in a story can determine what kind of world the author creates. The novels of Jane Austen typically cover a year or two of time, and in the course of that time, the seasons pass in regular order, each using up an appropriate amount of fictional space. The effect is of a regular and stable world, reflecting a stable society. Time in *Crime and Punishment* is highly unstable: nights and days go by without distinction, it's hardly ever possible to sense what day or hour it is; the chaos of time reflects the disordered mind of the character. The centrally instructive thing about this critical distinction is this: the passage of time in fiction is entirely in the writer's hands, and how you choose to manage time must have a narrative reason.

Other new (or very old, resharpened) tools have come from the recovery, by the Theory workers, of terms out of classical rhetoric, which they use to bare the very old abstract structures of apparently newly-forged statements—parabasis, peripeteia, proplepsis (and that's only the p's). I derive terms of art from the typology of Northrop Frye, which is neither New Criticism nor post-structuralism but *sui generis*—what his terms share with the others is that they are to be wielded not in search of value, or to crack the personal code of an author, but to understand the workings of *all* fiction, and thus may help writers understand what they are up to when they write stories. (It amazed me, when I started writing fiction in my twenties, how little I knew about how to go about it, though I had read countless stories.) These tools seem to me so flexible and useful that I insist my students understand, apply, and remember many of them. I think it's very likely that mine is the only Advanced Fiction workshop taught at university level that gives a final—all Multiple Choice.

And yet, though I believe that providing to students the most useful tools I can find, with which they can then do whatever they are capable of doing, is the best thing I can do as a teacher, I also know about the deep uses of fiction, for writer as for reader. The river of fiction has no beginning and will have no ending; it is coterminous with language (for all I know, it precedes it—the structures of story may be part of our mammalian brains) and to have drunk there and contributed to it in any way is self-justifying; it needs no excuse. When I first began teaching at Yale, the college paper interviewed me, and among other questions I was asked *Why do you write?* It was a question I'd heard before, but on this occasion an unexpected answer came from my mouth—I said that I write in order to win immortal fame. I am unlikely to do so, except in the same way that all parents are immortal merely in the fact of having continued the endless story of human life on earth. We are all immortal in reading and writing; the lies of fiction are necessary to the conscious lives we live.

2004

A MODERN INSTANCE:
MAGIC, IMAGINATION, AND POWER

*T*here was a time in my life when I was very afraid of magic.

There are countless ways to misunderstand this statement, or misread it anyway as it relates to my own experience. It demands firstly some definition of magic, the naming at least of a few categories or limits; all bare there, it contains at once too much and not enough. It would also require one to know that, though I have been writing books about the possibility of magic, of other worlds hidden inside of or containing this one, of intelligences around us who do not share our natures, I have never since early childhood believed in magic. (All young children do, of course; they believe that names have power over things, that ritual repetitions are binding, that our souls go forth in dreams.) I have a profound fondness for the intricacy and metaphorical reach of human systems such as astrology and alchemy, but I know that they—and associated magics like numerology and geomancy, and imitation sciences like homeopathy—are not in themselves effective. Either the guiding principles of alchemy and homeopathy are so, or the principles of modern physical chemistry are so: they can't both be.

The magic I came to fear—I first began to notice it at the time of the Jim Jones cult suicides, I was pursued by it in a series of dreams that are vivid to me still, and I came to recognize it almost like a witch-hunter by its smell when I came near it—was magic that claimed power over death, through resurrection or physical immortality, and mastery of other physical constraints accordingly. Of course the church I grew up in claimed power over death, and it never scared me, though it bored and repelled me at times; but over the course of centuries that church had surrendered (or allowed to lapse) its more *active* claims to be able to stop death, or raise the dead, settling instead for guaranteeing believers a good place among them in the other world.

I didn't believe that those cults and mages and hieratics who claimed those powers over death and the world actually possessed it. It was their power to compel belief that I found frightening. Many people I knew found it dismaying and unfortunate: I felt threatened by it in ways I have never understood.

That magic really does have power can't of course be denied. We all know that voodoo and witchcraft can kill their victims—though I'm quite sure that, despite the fears of ages, they can't affect horses and sheep. Their power is *intersubjective,* occurring between or among human consciousnesses, and it is this power I experienced. I was subject to bad magic *as though* it could work, while denying that it could. That is to say: I always knew that the intersubjective power of magic was great; I knew that in all times and places it had been used to gain power over hearts and minds and bodies too; I just didn't know that it could have power over someone who didn't believe in it, or believed he didn't believe in it—who knew its actual physics power to be nil. It was as though these wizards and their adherents were living in a different universe from mine and could inveigle me into theirs against my will and despite my unbelief.

It may strike you that I was astonishingly naive for someone who had given so much thought to these matters. Once, in those times of fearful confusion, I was in conversation with a friend who had no truck at all with magic or magic helpers, and I said, "I just don't know—are these powers simply *inside,* powers of the soul and mind, or are they maybe really powers *outside,* in the world? Which?" And he said "Both," which is indubitably so, and why couldn't I think of that?

Time and thought, and other people, and new paths appearing, all carried me away from the puzzlements and terrors I felt, without ever finally resolving them. One of those people was someone with a profound respect for magic, and a new way of conceiving it, as a power of the soul and a power in the world, who knew its history and grasped its principles with astonishing perspicacity, and who was a magician himself, a practicing magician—a good magician, my good magician; for an amazing and terribly brief time a mentor and way-maker: and it's he I would like to speak about.

I originally came to know of Ioan Culianu because of my interest in Giordano Bruno. I'd discovered Bruno long before, through Frances Yates, the British scholar who did so much in the 1960s to change our picture of the Renaissance and its mentalities. In her book *The Art of Memory*, which I picked up mostly because of the wonderful title, Bruno appears as a daring and extravagant figure who transformed a classical rhetorical tool into a magic system by which the mind was to gain vast new powers through the cultivation of an astrologically and mythologically founded mnemonic system. The astonishment I felt at this, that someone in the past could have thought so differently from myself about what the mind is and what it can do, was immensely suggestive to me. A huge historico-scientific magical-realist phenomenological epic opened its vistas before my eyes, which is something that I can sometimes nowadays regret, as perhaps some of my readers can as well.

It was mental power, or thought power, which at that time I conceived Bruno's system to be about; in my conception his mnemonics became a metaphor for the benevolent, harmless power I knew myself to possess—the power of vivid memory, the combinatory power of mentation, of things imagined so vividly they seem to be remembered rather than invented—in other words, the arts of fiction in general.

It was some years later, and after my dealings with magic, that I came across a book by Ioan Culianu that altered and complicated my vision of Bruno—darkened it, I might say, but *developed* it too like a photograph. The book was one that many have become aware of, I think, perhaps through people who like me have been influenced or touched by it. It was called *Eros and Magic in the Renaissance*,* and Giordano Bruno was a central exemplar, along with Marsilio Ficino, Faust, the author of the *Hypnerotomachia Poliphili*, and others. It made clear to me what the magicians of the Renaissance thought they were doing, and why it made sense, given their physics and their biology, and why these made sense given their cosmology; and it showed me a way to understand magic and the magical.

---

*The author's name appears on the book as "Ioan Couliano". The French publisher of the orignal altered the Romanian spelling of Culianu's name, as it admitted of an unfortunate pun in French.

Thinkers of the past were, in Culianu's vision, no less acute than thinkers of the present, no less psychologically astute; their insights are cast in terms incompatible with ours but are nonetheless often immediately recognizable to us. In Renaissance terms the physical body and the soul are entities of such radically different orders—a cosmogonical Jack Sprat and his wife—that they can communicate only through some intervening medium, which is the *spirit*—a sort of tenuous, thin, hot, shiny, fine substance composed of air and fire, highly volatile and reflective, that runs all through the body. What the body senses through the eyes and the ears is reflected in this spirit as in a mirror, and the soul, which can't perceive anything material, can see it, just as we can see the immaterial reflections in a mirror.

Thus, in the Renaissance, love melancholy was caused by images of a loved one entering in through the eye and getting loose in the spirit—invited in by lust, a hot temperament, a cold retaining temperament, whatever—and there taking over. So what the lover suffers from is not the fact of an unattainable beloved but only the *image* of the beloved that he can't expel. He becomes a robot, operated by this vampiric image, which he thinks connects him to the beloved, but (though it once might have) no longer does; he can no longer see or know the beloved, or anything else either except for this overmastering image that has infected him; his spirit is conquered, polluted, and sick, wandering (in Culianu's striking figuration) "those roads to nothingness, where bodies cast no shadow, and mirrors reflect nothing" *(Eros* 31).

Well, that's what I think too. It's what we all know is true about sick love. The science is strange but the conclusion is sound.

The questing spirits of that time, like Bruno, went on to draw very large conclusions from their premises, as we do from ours, and to project huge possibilities for altering human life with their techniques—as we do from ours. In his book Culianu examined at length a late unpublished work of Bruno's called *De vinculis in genera,* "On Bonds in General," which deals with the power of images that pass from one soul to another by means of the spirit, and what might be done by means of this power by a skilled operator.

In this tract, as Culianu dissected it, Bruno asserts that all tendencies or affections of our wills are reducible to two, aversion and desire, hatred and love; but hatred is itself only love in reverse, so the only bond of the soul is Love. *Vinculum summum, præcipium et generalissimum;* the highest, most excellent and most general bond. That's why Plato calls love the Great Dæmon, *dæmon magnus.* By love Bruno meant not warm feelings of approval or charity but the fire of *eros,* desire, whether for conquest or intellectual attainment or understanding or another person.

We can bind ourselves, or be bound. The magic operator uses *images* that bind: images, so constructed as to be charged with astral energy, can cause us to love or hate, fear or trust, be steadfast or dissolute. Images, built in the imagination *(phantasticum)* by the binder, enchainer or enchanter, sent forth as physical objects—amulets, seals, poems—or projected directly, from soul into soul. In fact we are all subject to such manipulations proceeding from the spirits of others; all of us do it all the time. The worker in magic is he who *consciously* uses the resources of his own heart, its fears and desires, to bring about the effects he wants, to seduce one soul or many at once, to cure or to control.

Bruno says that while individuals can be controlled by images tailored specifically to their individual astral natures, masses of men are actually more easily compelled by images that appeal to our general natures, the desires and fears we all share.

It's almost not necessary to notice how the claims and aims of this kind of magic—of which, as Culianu shows, Bruno was the sole unashamed and unembarrassed proponent in his time—descend to our world. While the practical aims of the old-time magician—to travel anywhere instantaneously at will, to observe what is happening at a distance, to have a vast infallible memory, to transform matter—have devolved to new technologies, "nothing," Culianu says, "has replaced magic on its own terrain, that of intersubjective relationships." Public relations, advertising, propaganda, information technologies, market research, tacit censorship, media control—all function exactly as Bruno says magic does: by the conscious manipulation of effective images of fear and desire. The magician develops in himself the erotically charged images that he understands can move others, and while yet remaining unmoved himself, projects these on others to bring about calculated effects: projects them through the star-generated aether through the power of magic mnemonics, in Bruno's terms; through fabulous and pervasive media in ours.

Bruno's theses were, in Culianu's opinion, more groundbreaking (except for the fact that almost no one knew of them) than Machiavelli's. Machiavelli never went beyond the common means of his day for achieving and holding on to power, the ancient ones of fraud and force. His innovation lay in a new moral stance: The priests and the Gospels teach us that we should not use such means, but in order to achieve things that we all agree to be good—stability, safety, a happy society—we must use them; so take your choice. Bruno's moral stance was exactly the same—here is a technique for mass manipulation which one can use and with it make men believe themselves happy, create a homogeneous society that is calm and governable, and, though swept with strange longings and fears, stable over time. Whether it is *right* to do this is not part of Bruno's study. Culianu adds, though, that Bruno holds out the possibility that the effective manipulator will also know how to free a bound soul, or maybe many souls, from such enchantment.

But is our modern Western state a true magician, Culianu asks, or "a sorcerer's apprentice who sets in motion dark and uncontrollable forces?" *(Eros* 105). He thought it was very hard to tell, but he distinguished between the magician state—such as the ones he came to live in in the West—and the police state, like the Communist Romania in which he grew up, from which he escaped. The police state, in order to defend a worn-out ideology in which no one believes, represses both freedom and the illusion of freedom, "changing itself into a prison where all hope is lost" *(Eros* 105). It is bound to perish. The magician state, on the other hand, can degenerate into a sorcerer state, providing only the illusion of satisfaction and possibility, keeping the controls hidden; its faults are too much subtlety and too much flexibility, an inability to propose radical solutions. "Yet the future belongs to it anyway," Culianu says; "coercion by the use of force will have to yield to the subtle processes of magic, science of the past, of the present, and of the future" *(Eros* 106).

Well! With this book in hand—it determined perhaps more than any other the thought-processes by which my work with Bruno and magic was shaped—I had a *vade-mecum* or spirit companion, an epopt, a psychopomp whom I could lean on, who made me laugh out loud as well with astonishment and delight. It provided for me a vision of magic and how it might be understood to work today, not merely as intersubjective magic—though never without an

A Modern Instance: Magic, Imagination, and Power

intersubjective component—but as a technology, one to which I as well as any soul might be subject. You might say that magic lies at the intersection of technology and subjectivity, even (risking overstatement) that it *is* that nexus. Magic is the science of the past, the present, the future because this nexus is permanent in human cognition and therefore in human action.

For another example, a story I had known before reading Culianu but could newly understand in this light: In the late 15th century the Abbot Trithemius of Sponheim, a fabled magician, produced for the Emperor Maximilian I a spectral vision of his dead wife, the famously beautiful Mary of Burgundy. (It's said of Mary that her skin was so fair and fine that when she drank red wine one could see it pass down her throat.)† Mary died at 25 in a riding accident, leaving Maximilian heartbroken and frozen in grief. To get him to return to his royal duties, Trithemius promised to conjure for him the spirit of Mary so the Emperor could see her once more; the only rule was that he could not speak to her. In a darkened room Mary duly appeared, in the very dress Maximilian knew her to have worn in life.

Now it's possible to class this story with a thousand others that no longer compel our wonder, even if the Emperor did attest to it himself—until we remember that Athanasius Kircher, the 17th century developer of the magic lantern, stated that Trithemius had already invented it 150 years before him. So maybe what Trithemius showed the Emperor was a slide show; and if so where was the magic? It lay, firstly, in the technology—in the *natural* magic of what Kircher called *Ars Magna Lucis et Umbræ*, the Great Art of Light and Shadow; and, secondly, in the manipulation of light and image in such a way as to move and heal a soul, Maximilian's; light itself being, in Trithemius's world-view, a quasi-immaterial entity that alone of all created nature could reach the soul directly. An image of a beloved, made entirely of light and memory: what could be more magical?

We all know the chestnut about how any sufficiently advanced technology will appear to be effective magic to those unfamiliar

---

† I have recently discovered that this was actually another Mary. [Author's note]

with it. I think this (really somewhat doubtful) apothegm at least deserves a corollary: any bypassed magic that was practiced for a long time by large numbers of people can be understood as an effective technology if we become familiar enough with it. That's the premise Ioan Culianu started with.

I came to know Ioan Culianu himself through a series of quasi-magical coincidences and synchronicities that never ceased as long as I knew him, which was not long. Jennifer Stevenson brought us together when she asked me to come to her Chimæra Conference in Chicago; when she asked me whom else I'd like her to invite, I mentioned Culianu, whom I'd just read; she found him right across town, at the University of Chicago, and found he was happy to come.

She encouraged me to write to him, which I did, and received a gracious and very flattering reply (he'd already read my books), with the news that he'd be in my neighborhood in Massachusetts very soon, could we get together? He was in Massachusetts with his friend and—I think at that point—his fiancée, Hilary Wiesner, whose family lived in Amherst, twenty minutes from me; he was visiting a professor of religion at Smith, Carol Zaleski, and her husband Phil, an acquaintance of mine, and yes, of course I'd love to have dinner with them: and he turned out to be not a craggy white-maned great-eyed philosopher-king but a man no older than me, no larger either, placid-seeming, pleasant-faced; his only sinister aspect was a pair of black-framed green-tinted glasses, but those turned out to have an explanation, he'd broken his usual ones.

From then on we met, wrote, talked on the phone. Like the mentor-tricksters of modern novels, he kept appearing, in a new guise, at every intellectual juncture I reached myself. I had become interested in Gnosticism—that's too mild a word, I was fascinated by, moved by, appalled by the Gnostic mythos, as I discovered it in the work of Hans Jonas. Oh? Well, Culianu had travelled with Jonas, knew him well, he was himself at work on a major reinterpretation of Gnosticism.* Mircea Eliade on magic, time, witches, the religious cosmos? Oh, Culianu was at the University of Chicago because of Eliade; he was in fact taking over the editing of a huge encyclopedia

---

* *The Tree of Gnosis*, Harper 1992

of comparative religion from the ailing Eliade; perhaps I could contribute to it, a piece on alchemy maybe. Travel to other worlds, worlds within worlds? His next book—would I like to see galleys?—was called *Out of this World*, and was about otherworldly journeys. Prague and the Golem? He would introduce me to his friend Moshe Idel, who was the leading scholar. Science fiction? He had written several short pieces and a novel; he was thinking of a time-travel story, perhaps we could collaborate . . .

I know that I'm not the only person on whom Culianu had the effect he had. Many who knew him recognized that he had the power of transforming the atmosphere in which he stood, charging it positively somehow (I apologize for this unscientific physics metaphor) and filling his interlocutors with a sense of possibility, of *their own* possibilities. The interpersonal power he projected was perhaps no different from the magic that Dale Carnegie used to sell: "There's a deep gnawing hunger that is rarely satisfied," said Carnegie, "the hunger to be appreciated, and the man or the woman who satisfies that can win friends and influence people and hold people in the palm of his hand." Well, that's real intersubjective power, and it's like Culianu's; I don't suppose Carnegie attributed his power to his huge heart's grasp of the astrological moment and the corresponding nature of his subject's astral body, but I'm not so sure about Culianu. He might have said—very nearly did say—that he used the means of Bruno and Bruno's forebears, and by those means attracted to him those he wished to attract, conquered where he wished to conquer, absorbed and mastered—or was seen to have mastered—vast masses of erudition in several languages at superhuman speed. I know he was deeply interested in Tarot, in synchronicity, in color symbolism, in the power of talismanic images.

How interested? As power *inside*, or as power *outside?* I think his magical thinking was a form of negative capability, what Keats defined as the power to hold contrary possibilities in the mind without any irritable striving after fact and certainty. I too know how to do this—in what Tolkien called the secondary creation, a work of fiction. He was capable of it in the mental and even the social and political realms he moved in, and as it does the poet, it gave him power. It even posed for him the questions that power poses, the very questions he addressed when considering Bruno.

Just when I met Culianu, the Communist regimes in Eastern Europe were falling apart. The first night we met, we talked of the end of the Romanian dictatorship. Culianu characterized the events in Romania as a plan by the Soviet KGB to eliminate the unpopular Ceausescus under the guise of popular reform, a plan which got out of hand and became a revolution, forcing the Communists to become, or appear to become, democrats in order to retain power. In the new regime, ultra-nationalism again became a political force, and the suppressing of enemies abroad—something Romanian Securitate had always taken seriously—continued on an even broader front.

Many of Culianu's American friends didn't know how involved he was in post-Communist Romanian public life, and how much danger he was in because of it. He continued publishing in *emigré* and underground papers his outspoken critiques of the regime and its bad magic. He told his students and friends—but not the police—that he thought he was being followed, and took out additional life insurance. Then in May 1992 he was shot in the head in the men's room of the divinity school at the University of Chicago where he had an office. He was forty-one years old. The crime is assumed to have been a political assassination, either by the pseudo-democrats of the new regime or the quasi-Fascist Old Guard exiles in America; it has never been solved.

I went to Chicago in the company of his Amherst fiancée to attend the memorial service the University held for him. In the course of those days she asked me to go with her to Culianu's apartment, which she had the duty of emptying. In a desk drawer she found and took out a large photo album, which she pondered what to do with. It was filled not with snapshots but with dozens of Polaroid pictures of Tarot card lay-outs in several shapes, each neatly dated, some with other notes. I was astonished. He kept all these? Sure, she told me. You have to have check on your predictions. What else are Polaroids for?

What remains to be understood, or explained, is why being in the presence of this practitioner of intersubjective magic did not make me afraid, or cause the mother to rise, or induce the creeps, as so many other manifestations had. Was it just that he was a good magician and not a bad one? At that conference in Chicago to which he came, where at late-night parties he laid out Tarot for us with striking results (when are they not?), I put forward the thesis at one point that all magic is bad magic: meaning it is always coercive, usually concealed, and always comprises a power to be used against others for gain or aggrandizement. Culianu not only disagreed, he seemed hardly to understand the remark. But I recently found my question rephrased very exactly by the Russian writer Victor Erofeyev in an article about Rasputin, the monk who dominated the Russian royal family with his power to prophesy and to heal, and who was also a relentless spiritual and sexual predator.[†] *The question about Rasputin*, says Erofeyev, *is not whether he was really a faith healer or a vampire. The question is whether the one who loves less always wins.*

I think that if my question had been put in those terms Culianu would have understood. Giordano Bruno said that in order to have power over others, the magician must cultivate within himself all the intensity of spiritual and physical desire, while at the same time remaining immune to it. He made no claim about whether this was right to do, only that he knew how to do it. So what I wanted to know is, is this the only way magic can work? Does the less love always win? I think Culianu would have understood, and I think his answer would have been a qualified No.

Intersubjective magic and physically effective magic lie along one axis, at the center of which is that nexus of technology and subjectivity of which I've spoken. The axis of good and bad magic lies in another direction, and comprises a different power, the power of binding at one extreme but of unbinding at the other. I think Culianu intended to use the powers he cultivated as Bruno promised they could be used: to free rather than to bind, to enable not only himself but those he loved and encountered to shadow forth, to embody, the magicians they could themselves be. In his last communication published in Romania he wrote that "Mankind has not yet found a remedy against death. Miracles though exist. Daring to form an idea leads to life ... Death is saying no to life and life is saying no to Death. Have the courage to say NO and you will rise on the third day."

[†] Erofeyev, Victor. "Rasputin Returns." *New York Review of Books* March 29, 2001

The question may finally be asked what this has to do with the general subject we are here to discuss, the fantastic in the arts; the fantastic being magic admitted to be illusion, and the arts likewise. It may seem banal to assert that art is a form of effective magic, really, and that the artist is a magician; but in the terms I have developed here, the terms of the Renaissance magicians, it might not be so banal. They thought that their natural magic could alter the material world, compel the forces that make the world as it is, and our natural magic (more successfully) does the same; but their *spiritual* magic aimed to achieve just what our media and communication arts can be shown to achieve: the trans-subjective projection of powerful and heart-changing images. Even the technologies of prose fiction, not unsubtle themselves, are potent enough to drive a Don Quixote mad, surely many more than one.

No, the question for us as artists is the question of good magic and bad. Powerful, indeed unforgettable, work can be done in art by mages who themselves remain unenchanted; the self-enchanted worker often fails disastrously to enchant anybody else. The question remains, a sort of meta-question beyond such successes and failures: how do we in our art unbind as well as bind? Does the less love always win? I don't know, though my answer is a qualified No. But it may be why I am myself so drawn to the metafictional. I want my readers to know my secrets too.

Lady Gregory somewhere tells the story of St. Patrick and the Druids, and how St. Patrick asked them, if they claimed to know so much, who made the world? And the Druids replied, The Druids made it. The great Zen masters, though—so I am given to understand—would from their high seats instruct their students, tease them, pose insoluble problems for them, abuse them even; until at length, after years maybe, the student would one day say "But you're just pretending! You don't know anything because there's nothing to know, there is no secret, you're master of nothing!" At which point, of course, the master would arise from his seat, and offer it with a bow to the graduate and new master.

2001

THE LABYRINTH OF THE WORLD AND
~ THE PARADISE OF THE HEART ~

[1]

I TAKE MY SOMEWHAT PECULIAR title from a short book written in 1623 by a once very well known thinker named Jan Andreas Komensky, known by the Latin version of his name as Comenius.

Comenius was a native of Bohemia, which was once a real country, part of what is now Czechoslovakia. He belonged to a mild and ecumenical Protestant sect called the Brethren, which was suppressed by the Catholic rulers of Czechoslovakia; Comenius spent his last years wandering from country to country attempting to advance his radical ideas of universal reform.

Comenius—like many of his contemporaries—was addicted to a pursuit that has claimed an inordinate amount of the mental effort of many of Western civilization's strongest minds; I don't know if it occurs widely in other civilizations, but in the West it forms a long and strange tradition. I'm talking about the imagining of utopias: new and better ways of organizing human life and society, different civilizations, without the flaws and limitations of the one the writer happens to live in, and more pleasing to its citizens or to God. Comenius called his own imagined possible civilization Pansophia, and all his life he projected plans for it: how its educational system might work, what its science and religion might be like, how it would foster the flowering of human abilities and human happiness.

At the same time, Comenius was fascinated by another mode of thinking, equally popular at various junctures in Western history: the possibility that civilization—the world as it is, society, the human ecology—might be rotten to the core and about to come to an end altogether. When Christians like Comenius hold views, or feel feelings, of this kind, they are called *millenarians*: because in

Christian dogma when God brings this wicked world (that is, our human society) to an end, it will be succeeded by a millennium in which Christ will rule over a perfected earth and reformed humankind.

What I would like to do in the time given me here is to reflect somewhat on these different impulses which Comenius felt—that there is a possible civilization to be built, far better than the one we know, in which human beings can live fully, happily, and at peace; and, on the other hand, that the world which human beings have so far managed to make is hopeless, that it can't survive, that it is even now on its last legs and foundering.

Our topic is civilization—but not the civilizations we have built, or even the idea of civilization as such; our topic might be described as the dream of civilization. In Comenius's terms, the real civilization we have built—human society as it is—is the labyrinth of the world: the sad, meaningless, hurtful failure we have made out of our common life, to which we can owe no allegiance, and which in any case can't last long. At the center of this labyrinth is the paradise of the heart, the solitude where better worlds can be conceived, and where the happy certainty is born that they can be achieved as well.

These two images, which Comenius has opposed so beautifully, have been a constant in our imagination for centuries. The fact that no utopian system, no new plan for civilization, has ever been able to be established as its projectors imagined it, doesn't keep people from continuing to imagine new ones; the fact that our rotten old world never does quite collapse or come to an end, but just goes on building on its past, has not stopped people from imagining its imminent and total breakdown. Millenarian and utopian ideas are such a permanent fixture of our thinking about ourselves and our civilization that, if they were the obsessions of an individual, a psychoanalyst would suspect that they mean more than they seem, that they express deep and unacknowledged needs and fears. I think they do. I think that the opposed realms of Comenius's little book—the labyrinth of the world and the paradise of the heart—are not truly opposed; I think they are simply two aspects of a single undertaking, or attempt: the attempt to cancel out the complexities and ambiguities of the civilizations we are born with, and to live, instead, in simpler possibilities.

[2]

The one thing everyone knows about Utopia is that it was a place imagined by Thomas More, and that its name is a subtle pun in Greek: "topia" is derived from the Greek word for "place", and the "u" in front of it might mean "not"—not-a-place, Noplace—or it might be "eu", meaning "good", as in euthanasia and eugenics: Goodplace. An imaginary good place, then; an island that doesn't exist but whose mode of life is the best that Thomas More could imagine—a model for how we all might live.

The other thing that most modern people who know about Thomas More's invented place are sure of is that they would not want to live there. Life in Utopia seems to us today horribly restricted, programmed, unfree; the authorities are intolerably bossy and interfering; there is work and satisfaction but not much fun. Everyone is happy wearing the same sensible clothes, eating communal meals, participating in the state religion. Marriages are arranged, and child-rearing is closely prescribed.

Thomas More seemed to think—this is my feeling, anyway—that mankind's most basic needs are for safety, control, and regularity. Maybe this is not surprising when we consider the society in which More was living, the society described in J.K. Huizinga's wonderful book *The Waning of the Middle Ages*: a time of extremes—terrible cruelties and wild outbursts of religious enthusiasm, extremes of poverty and costly display, tyranny and neglect, people of every social condition in harm's way most of the time. Remember, Thomas More himself was to be executed by King Henry VIII after a dispute about religion.

So Thomas More evidently had a very different idea of what human fulfillment was about than we would hold today. And the same is true of most of the hundreds, possibly thousands, of Utopias that have succeeded Thomas More's. The fact is that to imagine a Utopia—a good place where any and all human beings would be glad to live—is actually to make a statement about what human beings are like. To construct a Utopia, you define human beings in a certain way, and then invent a setting appropriate for them.

When people find a Utopian scheme convincing or intriguing, what they are actually convinced by is the picture of humankind that it presents; when the general picture we have of what humankind is like changes, or deepens, or lightens or darkens, the old Utopias designed to contain and satisfy the old humankind cease to be convincing. In the hundred years between the appearance of More's little book and the appearance of Comenius's, the conception of humankind and the place of human beings in the universe changed radically in the European intellectual community, and so did the utopias which radical thinkers designed for them. If Thomas More's Utopia would be unpleasant for modern people to live in, the wild utopias imagined by the Baroque projectors of the next century are impossible to imagine living in at all. This is because they mostly depended on systems of magical sympathies in order to work—just as a utopia imagined today might depend on nuclear energy.

People who are given to designing utopias are often people who are easily swept up in big notions that explain the basic connections of the universe in a new way. They glimpse the possibility that if human societies could somehow also be connected in those basic ways, if human societies could be properly aligned with the physical universe, then societies would work just as the universe does, spontaneously and perfectly. (A modern thinker who held that view and whom you will have heard of is Buckminster Fuller.) In the sixteenth century, the big notion that intrigued the designers of utopias was the notion that man—the basic human being—is a microcosm of the universe at large; that the same forces that operate in the universe, that make the planets revolve, that cause plants to grow and the sun to burn, operate also within the human body and soul, and produce the same effects. The forces and principles which excited them, and which they thought were the operative ones in the universe, were a very peculiar collection indeed, entirely different from the forces and principles we might consider basic.

There were, first of all, the stars—not the stars we know about, but the starry principles of astrology, the twelve signs of the zodiac and the characters of the seven planets that travel within them. The influence of the heavens was thought to permeate totally the physical earth and the body and mind of human beings. Then there was the geometry of the solar system—which as far as these thinkers knew was the entire universe, with the distant background of the other stars. They believed that the circles, angular motions, geometrical relations, that obtained among the heavenly bodies had to be regular—that is, reducible to perfect circles, squares, triangles and so on—and that those same geometrical regularities also obtained within the microcosm—the human body and spirit. It was thought that the human mind had a special affinity for such figures, a natural disposition. Think of Leonardo's drawing of a man inscribed on a circle and a square.

So these utopias were very different from the plain-style utopia of Thomas More. They were designed to reflect the whole universe in small. Their microcosm men and women were to be housed in cities or palaces that had the geometrical regularities of the solar system, which means they were often conceived as pyramids, or spheres, or pyramidal towers within square walls within circular walls. They were often designed to be bathed alternately in different colors of light, appropriate to the good planetary and stellar influences the designer wanted to attract. Their religions were not the mild civil religion of Thomas More's island but extravagant, colorful affairs usually combining mystical Christianity with invocations of the stars through music, geometrical dance and so on. Something of what they may have been intended to look like can be seen today at Versailles, for the designers of that astonishing palace were influenced by the thinking of these utopians.

Another thing that distinguishes these thinkers of the Baroque age—which is also the age of Comenius—from Thomas More is their ambitions. More's island of Utopia might have been meant as an example, a good idea, a model of how a good community might work; but the thinkers of Comenius's period thought always of universal, world-wide total reform—which is exactly the title of a tract put out in those years by writers calling themselves Rosicrucians: *The Universal Reformation of the Whole Wide World*.

This utopian ambition for total renewal continues from then on throughout our intellectual history. When the Baroque combination of geometrical regularities, astral powers, and mystical Christianity gets old, utopian thinkers take up other big ideas. Universal language, new science, industrial power, technology, personal fulfillment, sexual freedom, evolution, all have been seized on by thinkers who see in them new programs for reorganizing human society more successfully. But always this conviction animates them, that nothing less than total renewal will do; the whole of past human culture has been a mistake, and has to be cleared out of the way, or overgrown, or supplanted—human society as it stands is a total failure, it will collapse of its own contradictions very soon and the new form of civilization had better be ready.

This seems to me to be an important distinction to make within the whole utopian tradition: between the modest proposals and the total programs. People who design model communities, or plan cities to be more humane or more convenient or more beautiful, or think of ways to combine a work environment with a living environment, are often called utopian; but they aren't the sort of utopian that interests me. The ones who interest me are the ones like those of the age of Comenius, who could entertain nothing less than a total renewal of society, a wholly other civilization arising out of the husk of the abandoned and collapsed old civilization. It is this *total* aspect of utopian thinking that puzzles, intrigues, annoys me, makes me laugh, makes me marvel. The philosopher Henri Bergson defined the comic as arising from the imposition of geometrical form on the formless contents of consciousness—and maybe that's what my utopians are attempting to do, and it may be why their visions, universal and total though they attempt to be, so often seem to be so comically limited, and inhabited by cartoon figures or stick men and not real people.

All utopias differ from real human societies or civilizations in containing less than real societies do. Real societies are like immense and tangled forests, young trees climbing out of the mulch of dead ones, a bewildering and unnecessary profusion of leaves, vines, bushes, animals, flourishing growth and sickly growth and deadwood; nothing is cleaned away or tidied up, because every part of it is too busy being alive and striving for a bit of light. Utopias tend to put a premium on tidiness; if you are going to construct a forest from scratch, the temptation is to plant the trees in regular rows, like the pine plantations around reservoirs, and to keep the undergrowth down. Utopias tend to have fewer possibilities for both good and bad—less vice and crime and suffering, less waste, less tragedy; but also, typically, fewer trivial amusements, fewer fads and fashions, fewer ways of making a living or gaining social power or winning love, fewer institutions in general.

In fact, the more highly detailed and complete a thinker's plans are, the less his projected utopia seems to have in it. And this thinness is even more evident when it comes to the people whom the utopia is supposed to contain, who are supposed to flourish there: the more their daily lives are described, the more satisfactions and occupations they are described as having, the more unreal they seem to be. Remember, the projector of a utopia is in fact making a statement about what human beings are like; the more detailed his statement, the more incomplete it seems as a description of the human beings we in fact know, including ourselves. Whoever these happy, thriving folks are, singing on their way to work, joyfully participating in the social rituals the author has thought up—whoever they are, we think, they aren't me, or anyone I know or *want* to know. They are fictions: in other words they are deliberately—though not always consciously—made simpler than real people, more easily describable and graspable, more easily satisfied. And therein, I think, lies the appeal of utopias: the appeal not for readers, or for society, which has always been unwilling to go very far toward establishing them, but for those who think them up.

A poignant example of this which I have studied is the spectacle presented by the New York World's Fair of 1939, which was consciously intended by its designers to be a kind of utopia—a place in which visitors could experience a possible world of the future, a good place that could be built by science, social engineering, and human cooperation. All the new technologies that could be deployed in making this new world were on display, and the great hopes for them asserted as facts: there was television, and synthetic fabrics like rayon, and plastics in many forms, and streamlined trains and planes and dirigibles—in fact everything was streamlined, whether it moved or didn't. At the heart of this fair, within its geometrical theme center, was presented a model city of the future—Democracity—a rationally planned metropolis with satellite suburbs, a modern port, skyscrapers, landing fields for autogiros and Zeppelins, no slums, no sleazy strip, no abandoned inner city. In fact, the most noticeable thing about Democracity was that the past—that is, the present of those who came to look at it—had vanished entirely, swept away by the clean bright future coming into being. Who was to live in Democracity? All around the model city were projected the figures of the citizens of the future—the workers, the farmers, the managers, the wives and children—and their voices were heard, cheerful and strong, talking about the cooperation and honest hard work that would have to go into making a decent world for themselves and their kids.

The World's Fair was not all utopian; there was an honest and not contemptible effort by its designers to understand the technological future which really was coming, and to prepare fairgoers to be able to live in it. But the extravagant hopefulness of it, the confident expectation of a scientific wonderland where nothing is impossible and society is continually reshaped by new machines, new discoveries, new techniques, and robots or nuclear energy or computers do all the work and provide for all human needs, and simple-minded human beings are endlessly willing to discard the past and endlessly delighted with more and faster ways of traveling—this is what people at the time were struck by; and it descends to us, of course, in the form of science fiction. When people who don't read very much science fiction refer to "a science-fiction sort of world" they generally mean those towering Buck Rogers cities entwined in elevated highways and swarming minijets that were on view at the Fair.

Well, it's easy to laugh at the World's Fair of 1939, at the General Motors "Futurama" for instance, a 1939 vision of the wonderful world of 1960, full too of clean cities, huge highways, new cars, friendly happy people, the past having vanished; it's impossible not to feel that the future the Fair pictured was not only not ever possible but never really desired either, even though the fictional farmers in overalls, workers in coveralls, wives in shirtwaist dresses, seem deliriously happy to be there.

But think now of the real world in which this vision was presented. 1939: the longest economic depression in history had not yet entirely lifted; America had been stalled for a long time, and social injustice remained entrenched and intractable; slums, infant mortality, poverty, danger of a degree that would appall a modern American, were facts of life. In Europe irrational and violent social movements, Nazism, Fascism, utopian visions of a different and potent kind, were forcing the world into a war that could only be more catastrophic, more destructive, than the Great War that had ended only twenty years before. In fact that new war began the year the fair opened.

The world was a dark labyrinth in 1939; if there was ever a year in which millenarian fears were justified—fears that the world, the

Labyrinth of the World, Paradise of the Heart 45

world as we knew it, was coming to an end—it was that year. And in that year was built this imaginary good place, geometrical and rational, the World of Tomorrow as they called it, which strikes us now as comically limited and very unlikely, but which can also be seen as a paradise of the heart, not really a *proposal* at all but simply a longing: for cleanliness and health and safety and a little ease in a world that did not offer them generously.

Do we have a clue here to the motive force in utopian thinking? Let's look again at the world in which Jan Andreas Comenius lived, the world in which he conceived his Pansophia, in which he wrote his *Labyrinth of the World and the Paradise of the Heart.* I said he was a Czech, a native of Bohemia, which was a primarily Protestant country, but a part of the Holy Roman Empire, a Catholic institution. The crown of Bohemia was elective—that is, the Czechs could decide who they wanted to be king, though the list of possible candidates was pretty short, and in fact the Emperor was almost always chosen King of Bohemia as well. But in 1620, fearful that the rights of the Protestant majority were about to be taken away, the Czechs rebelled; their electors refused to give the crown to the Emperor, and instead elected a Protestant prince from far west along the Rhine. When the Emperor's representatives came to Prague to protest, the Czechs threw several of them out a high window—a historical event known ever since as the Defenestration of Prague.

At that time the terrible Protestant-Catholic conflicts which had torn apart Christian civilization in the previous century had abated momentarily, though the struggle for what we might call hearts and minds went on furiously; neither the Catholic powers nor the Protestant ones were willing to live in a divided Christendom, and were armed to the teeth and convinced of the sanctity of their cause. In this charged atmosphere dozens of schemes were being put forward for reuniting Christian civilization; many of the Baroque utopian schemes I have talked about were at bottom attempts to reestablish Christendom and spread it around the world in a revitalized form. Among the most bizarre were the alchemical fantasies of a group of Protestant writers and thinkers—they attached the name "Rosicrucian" to their early manifestoes—who served the Protestant prince whom the Czechs so boldly elected their king.

Now a prime requisite for a Baroque utopia was that it had to win the support of some powerful prince in order to have any hope of succeeding. Comenius, for instance, was always trying to get one monarch or another interested in his schemes. Remember this is the age described in your history texts as the Age of Absolutism; kings were gathering huge autocratic powers, and this was seen as a good thing by most thinkers. The Rosicrucian utopians could suppose that the new King of Bohemia would be such a monarch; that after restoring the rights of the Czechs he might go on to become Emperor himself, and perhaps—if the right cosmic powers and true religious impulses could be combined in him and his servants—be the means by which a Christian utopia could be established.

It was not to be. If Bergson is right that comedy results from the imposition of geometric form on the formless contents of consciousness, then it might be equally true to say that tragedy results from the attempted imposition of utopian perfection on the formless contents of history. The new King of Bohemia proved to be both feckless and inflexible, and his support, cosmic and otherwise, quickly evaporated. The Catholic Emperor, supported by the Pope, mobilized against him, and easily defeated him in a single battle in 1620. The Bohemian Protestant church was not only deprived of its former rights, it was ruthlessly crushed and expunged, its adherents exiled, executed, imprisoned. A harsh Catholic supremacy was imposed on the Czechs that would last for centuries. The destruction of free Bohemia was the opening act in a Europe-wide war that would last for thirty years and be more terrible, more disruptive of civilian life and economy, more corrosive to humane values—more destructive of whatever we mean by civilization—than any war up until the twentieth century. Comenius and his fellow-Protestants were only a handful among the refugees and casualties engendered.

It was in the years of that defeat that Comenius wrote his book *The Labyrinth of the World and the Paradise of the Heart*. The hero of that little book, wandering in the labyrinth of failing civilization, is offered books full of formulas for the magic restoration of society, boxes of alchemical prescriptions for happiness, Rosicrucian secrets: but the wanderer finds that all the books and boxes are empty. So Comenius understood just how much false hopes for renewal are part of the labyrinth, part of the problem; but his own utopian schemes, which he never abandoned, were still, in his view, the solution. What we have to ask is how much the utopian impulse itself contributed to the harm done civilization by the Thirty

Years' War. We have to ask whether the utopian impulse itself, in its desire to simplify society and escape from the ambiguities of history and human nature, not only does no good, but does active harm as well.

I think, in this connection, again, of 1939, and that huge silly sad World's Fair, which was to promote world peace through scientific and technological progress. The Czechs had a pavilion at the World's Fair, but by the time the Fair opened, free Czechoslovakia had already been overrun by another absolutist power, the German Nazi empire. The Czech pavilion at the Fair stood as a sort of dumb reminder to the happy fairgoers visiting the utopian World of Tomorrow: a reminder of the power of history, and the intractability of human nature, and the realities of power. On its walls was carved a prophecy: "After the tempest of wrath has passed, the rule of thy country will return to thee, O Czech people." The words were written by Jan Andreas Comenius, three hundred years before.

[3]

History, James Joyce said, is a nightmare from which I am trying to awaken. The utopian thinker imagines himself to be shouting *Wake up!* to a sleeping world; the utopian—however impossible his schemes are—usually considers himself in the nature of a critic, setting up a standard of human possibility against which the failures of actual civilized life can be measured. He can claim that even if his schemes can never be realized, they will stand as a reproach, a spur toward betterment on the part of those who are able to change things in a more limited way. But it seems to me that something different actually animates the imaginers of utopias.

I said that the millenarian impulse—the sense that history is a nightmare, and we are all about to awaken—is not different from the utopian one, that they are both aspects of the same attempt, the attempt to escape from the ambiguities of history and human nature into simpler possibilities. What I mean is this: if history is a nightmare, if the world—our human world—really is a labyrinth with no exits, if the civilization we have made is a total failure and about to be written off (by God, by technological innovation, by revolution) then we are under no obligation to try to make it better in a practical or day-to-day way; we are under no obligation to be engaged as citizens of the society we live in; in fact we are under a negative obligation to distance ourselves from it, and bend our minds on the new world that is to come.

So millenarian fantasies are justification for utopian ones: if you can convince yourself that this civilization is washed up, finished, a nightmare of meaningless suffering, then you are justified in entertaining the total renovation of a utopia. You can elaborate your new world endlessly in the quiet of your heart, and still feel that you are criticizing society in a useful way and helping to change it. But what I think you are doing is something different. I think you are creating a fiction.

More than social criticism, more than proposals for change or philosophies of human happiness, the great utopian projects are enormous and highly original fictions, usually unconstrained by plots or "character development" or the twists and turns of the standard fiction of the age in which they are written. The great utopian projectors of the 17th and 18th and 19th centuries are engaged in something which writers of literary fiction have only dared to do in the modernist twentieth century: refashioning the world into fiction, replacing it with imagined worlds of their own, and peopling them with adams and eves who could exist nowhere else. I think the impulse to create utopias is not different from the impulse to create new worlds within fiction; both are aspects of a human need that is not often recognized, but which in my opinion is basic to our natures, like the need for order and for love: I mean the need for possibility. In the labyrinth of the world there is constant *change*—meaningless flux, one damned thing after another; it's in the paradise of the heart that possibilities are realized.

I know something about the impulse to create fictions, especially of that total kind; I have often been surprised by the intensity of my need for other possibilities, for worlds different in their nature from the one I live within. The readers and writers of science fiction and fantasy stories gather periodically in big conventions, and I have sometimes attended them, and found myself in the company of people with whom I seem to share very little except this need, as though I were at an AA meeting or a revival. I imagine that in such company the utopian projectors of the past would feel quite comfortable.

For the utopian impulse, as I noted, descends into science fiction; in science fiction novels is an endless array of other possibilities, *Worlds of If* as the old science fiction. magazine title put it. There is the old-fashioned World-of-Tomorrow sort of future—funny to think of a future as old-fashioned, but there it is—and there is a huge number of negative or anti-utopias as well. It is to the credit of science fiction writers that they have seen the contradiction in utopias—that the more totally imagined they are, the less they seem to contain, and that to live in one as a whole human being and not a utopian's stick figure would not be paradise but hell. Science fiction has come up with a term to describe these imagined societies, where everyone is compelled to be happy and no one is; they are called dystopias—*dys* meaning bad or wrong in Greek, so Badplace or Wrongplace. The term lacks the neat pun of the original, but it will do. Aldous Huxley's *Brave New World* was one of the earliest, and best, of these visions; thousands have followed.

The millenarian impulse also descends to science fiction, of course; science fiction novels are so often set in collapsed, failed, brutal, bombed-out societies, societies riven by awful plagues or destructive wars or environmental poisons, that the destroyed or failed world has become a trope, a commonplace, a cliché, like the shepherds and springtime of a pastoral romance. You know the kind of thing I mean: the *Mad Max* movies, *Blade Runner*. Science fiction, like the utopian literature it descends from, often seems to be warning us against these dangers, or satirizing the failings of our society or our human nature, or teaching us how to be different; but I think that such fiction is chiefly indulging in possibilities for their own sakes. It's interesting to observe that the modern consumers of utopias—the readers of science fiction—seem not to care whether they are of the u- or the dys- form, or of the millenarian kind, so long as there are lots of them. Possibilities are what is desired, not necessarily either good or bad, only different from what is.

What use, then, is this yen for possibility, that is unsatisfied by other countries, other peoples, other times and places, and needs whole new worlds to satisfy it, worlds complete (or seemingly complete) in every detail? Is it truly a human trait, or is it the ordinary human—even mammalian—taste for novelty and for new experience, simply exacerbated, distended, a bad habit, a neurotic symptom?

I was once asked by someone who had read my books why the futures I imagined in them were all bad—that is, why the societies I pictured were all failed or failing ones. I didn't have an answer; I had not consciously created only failed societies for my fictions to take place in. I began to ponder the fact. I saw that there was another trait which all of them seemed to share: that within the failed or shattered society I pictured there was the germ of a renewal, an unexpected hope, a chance for a new world, a new world growing unexpectedly at the center of the old one, like a bird within a spotted egg. As I have gone on working I have felt myself over and over again drawn to this double picture, of an old and dying world, and a new world within it trying to be born; and I found the same double impulse not only in the utopian projects I have described and in the fictions of other writers like myself, but in religious imagery and ritual and in potent political visions as well.

It's my belief—I am not able to prove it, or even about to try, and since I am not really a scholar or a historian I don't have to; making suggestive remarks is more my job—it's my belief that there are historical moments, moments when change seems inevitable but somehow refuses to happen; when the nature of humanity seems to be expanding with incredible rapidity, like an infant in a spurt of growth, finding new powers, coming out of a shell; when the irrational cruelties and stupidities of our society seem to have grown insupportable, and there is the euphoric certainty that they must bring society itself to an end. And I think that such moments might excite the utopian faculty, so to speak; inflame the organ, if there is one, that makes new worlds. I know that the late 1960s seemed to be such a time; that was the time when I discovered in myself the euphoria of new-world-making and old-world-destroying (on paper, of course); that was the time too, I often remember, when Czechoslovakia once again glimpsed the possibility of freedom, of self-realization, of humane independence, only to be suppressed again by an enormous armed empire, which was concerned only with the realities of power.

But what is most important to remember is that the ruthless empire that suppressed the Prague Spring of 1968—the Soviet Union—was itself born out of a utopian impulse in 1917. So was the Third Reich of Adolph Hitler, a utopia which if it had not been tried out by force on living people would seem to us among the most ridiculously limited and unreal of all utopias. For that matter, the Holy Roman Empire that crushed the Czechs in 1620 had begun as a utopian dream; it was to be the wicked old Roman Empire reborn and baptized and perfected.

I approach the very tentative conclusions I am able to reach: that the utopian impulse is not social criticism but the furthest reach of the impulse to construct fictions; that it is therefore most appropriately employed when, as in science fiction, it is restricted to the imaginary and kept from being imposed like a grid or a griddle on the living flesh of human beings; that we may never learn to restrict it in that way, and so will have to suffer the consequences, which consequences are called by us the history of our Western civilization—its empires and dream empires and gospels; and that, when all is said and done, we could probably not construct civilizations at all if our minds and hearts were not the sort to create the anti-civilizations called utopias as well.

The utopian dreamer rejects the world, it is a dark labyrinth; he finds in the paradise of the heart a new and better world. If today we look into his old schemes, re-experience his dream-world, we cannot help imagining his surprise if he could see the old world still in existence centuries on, still claiming at least some of the love and allegiance of its citizens, ourselves; he would be even more surprised to find that his own dream world, though no one any longer wants to bring it to realization, has become itself a cherished part of the heritage of our civilization, our mixed-up and untamed civilization—that hurtful, imperfect, all-too-human civilization *he* could not abide.

1986

FIVE WRITERS AND SOME OTHERS

ROBERT LOUIS STEVENSON

Robert Louis Stevenson and the Dilemma of an Uncritical Readership

*I*T WAS THE INTENTION OF the organizers of this centenary festival to invite both Stevenson scholars and non-specialists whose work has led them to be interested in Stevenson. I am not a scholar, of Stevenson or any other topic; but certainly it is my work that has led me to be interested in Stevenson. My interest is not nostalgic or bound up with the private pleasures of youthful reading, because I didn't read Stevenson when I was young. I knew verses from *A Child's Garden*. I saw and was deeply affected by the Disney version of *Treasure Island* with Robert Newton. But what I read was *Gods, Graves and Scholars*, and *Kon-Tiki*, and *Sons of Sinbad*, and Lowell Thomas in Tibet. In adventure stories, I preferred fact to fiction. I still do.

I began to read Stevenson as a grown-up, for professional reasons. I needed to learn how to write a story. It amazed me, beginning seriously to write long fictions, how little, despite a lifetime of reading them, we know how to set about writing one when the compulsion arises. I chose Stevenson not exactly at random to teach me; I divined that his were the qualities I needed, and perhaps they were, though to what extent I did or could adopt them is a question. I also came to admire profoundly qualities of his work which I could no more steal than I could the Elgin Marbles or a Turner sunset.

I admired Stevenson; I did more than that, I did what we are not to do with the characters we encounter in books—I *identified with* him. I identified with a writer whose deepest and most original motives arose from early childhood. I identified with a man of outwardly sunny disposition and elusive inward darkness. I identified with someone able to be described as at once slovenly and dandified, who had the habit of looking at himself in every mirror he passed. And I identified with his dilemma as a writer: that the kinds of stories he felt compelled to write were just those which a large and greedy readership were eager to read.

Why do I call this a dilemma? For most writers it would be a piece of sensational good luck, and certainly Stevenson in one sense flourished because of it. He died before the full implications of the dilemma were brought home to him—this is my personal interpretation—and yet they are apparent in *Weir of Hermiston* and his plans for completing it. And he discerned it clearly enough in some of its aspects. Here is a letter I first read quoted by John Noble in his illuminating preface to a collection of essays about Stevenson:

> What the public likes is work (of any kind) a little loosely executed; so long as it is a little wordy, a little slack, a little dim and knotless, the dear public likes it; it should (if possible) be a little dull into the bargain. I know that good work sometimes hits; but, with my hand upon my heart, I think it is by accident...

"I do not write for the public," he says. "I write for money, a nobler deity; and most of all for myself, not perhaps more noble, but both more intelligent and nearer home." And after bewailing the "bestiality of the beast whom we feed," he concludes, therefore: "There must be something wrong with me, or I would not be popular."

There must be something wrong with me, or I would not be popular. This can be read as simply the common snobbism of the period (common in other periods too) that the mob is incapable of appreciating the good and the beautiful and that great artists are bound to be scorned and ignored. But I would offer another interpretation: Stevenson was perceiving that if his works were popular with the consumers of adventure and romance novels, then perhaps his conception of the sort of book he thought he was writing was mistaken. There was no way for Stevenson to know for sure, but the enthusiasm of large numbers suggested that his work might in fact be—might necessarily be—more like the slack and knotless work he despised than he had hoped.

This uncomfortable possibility would have been reinforced by a comparison of his own work with work in the same line as his, equally or nearly as popular as his, but much worse by the standards Stevenson held to. "His" public—the public he shared with Rider Haggard and a dozen less memorable names—evidently didn't *mind* if the sort of books it liked were well written or highly finished; but it certainly didn't need them to be. Like a drunk capable of appreciating equally the one quality he seeks both in a vintage Bordeaux and a pint of discount vodka, readers of romance knew what they wanted, and knew when they had it. And if Stevenson's most devoted readers made no functional distinction between his works, which they loved, and other books, which they also loved but which were to Stevenson so evidently inferior, then was the distinction a real one? Simply to dismiss their, the dear public's, devotion as misguided wouldn't do, for Stevenson's dilemma was precisely this: that whatever else he wanted from, or in, the writing he did, he recognized himself as one of them; he wanted what they wanted. He wrote, he says, for himself; and what he himself wanted to write was romances. He himself suffered from the craving he satisfied.

At the time I was taking my lessons from Stevenson, I was beginning to publish work in certain modern genres of romance, fantasy and science fiction. There were, I suppose, clever career reasons for these choices, but at bottom it was because, wherever my imagination went, wherever I sent it, it tended to return with stories and situations of a certain kind. Only when I read Northrop Frye's study *The Secular Scripture* did I learn that the stories and motifs that I found within myself with such effort, always dredging up the same ones with such a thrill of discovery, were, however they had come to me, the permanent features of that body of Western writings definable as romance. Dangerous journeys in search of treasure or knowledge or lost identity. Descents into underworlds of confusion, repetition and dream, and upward journeys into integration, knowledge, community. Riddling prophecies, which prophesy the very journey undertaken to solve them. An abandoned or stolen home recovered; brothers and sisters reunited. I was writing romances, and there was a readership for them, certainly not as large as the readership for Stevenson's romances even relatively speaking, but a readership that is easier, nowadays, to gain and hold. There is a reason for that, and it has to do with the nature of romance, and the hunger of readers for it.

Stevenson can be seen as standing, with his readers, at the dawn of an age of popular literature whose noon has passed, but which is certainly the one we live in: where much of the business of most publishers and writers is to determine specific readerly appetites, and satisfy them. As in the creation and marketing of other consumer products, the marketers of fiction have been able to discriminate ever more finely among shades of need—like the proprietors of the best kind of brothel—and thus to present work that has been distilled down to solely the elements that will meet each need. It is likely that the consumers of certain genres of romance today are literally incapable of comprehending work written in certain other genres: all the integument common to all fiction, which still took up a good deal of all novels in Stevenson's day, has been skived off—no orientation is seen to be necessary, readers would not have bought a book that has a cover like this, a title ditto, and endorsements ditto, unless they already knew what they would get, and why they wanted it.

This is perhaps most true of those branches and sub-branches of the romance genres now being published under the rubric of fantasy and science fiction, which almost no one reads except those who read almost nothing else. These are intensely committed readers; theirs is not a simple sweet tooth for a certain kind of fiction; it is more like a sustaining addiction, it is the madness of Quixote. They will hug to themselves the books that meet their needs, and reread them till they fall apart. They will keep them in print by their demand; they will not suffer them to vanish.

These devotees like to gather together in large and small conventions where they meet each other and the writers who supply them with the books they need to read. We who attend these gatherings may share nothing else with one another except what draws us together, like the people at an AA meeting, or a revival. My greatest difficulty with my fellows in this fold is that though I know why I am among them I cannot bear to read most of the books they treasure. Many of these readers rate my books just as highly, they have been just as moved and exalted by them, as by books I have not been able to read more than a few pages of. "You," one or another of these ardent fans will tell me, "are one of my two favorite writers;" and I have learned not to ask who the other is. I fear sometimes that what is centrally interesting to readers in what I have written is not that which is special to it, what I most prize in it, but only what it shares with a whole class of fiction.

And that is why I identify with Stevenson, or why (as you may well be thinking) I project my own dilemma onto him: I believe that the kinds of stories Stevenson genuinely and wholeheartedly wanted to write were the kinds of stories that many many readers were eager to read, but that he wanted to write them for reasons different from the reasons the public—his fans—wanted to have them.

What reasons? Stevenson's writing on the subject of romance carries a tone more passionate than but similar to the tone of openhearted and smiling delight, just tinged with condescension, that he takes in writing about eccentric acquaintances or favorite dogs, and his modest manly populism might disguise as much as reveal what was most important to him in the sort of books he liked to read, and believed he wanted to write. The qualities he strives for are connected, he says, to how and why he read books as a boy: "We read stories in childhood, not for the eloquence of character or thought, but for some quality of the brute incident." The great writer of such stories, he says, shows us "the realization and apotheosis of the daydreams of common men:"

> His stories may be nourished with the realities of life but their true mark is to satisfy the nameless longings of the daydream. The right kind of thing should fall out in the right kind of place; the right sort of thing should follow... The threads of the story come from time to time together and make a picture in the web; the characters fall from time to time into some attitude to each other or to nature, which stamps the story like an illustration.

Achieving this impact seems to be in part a matter of leaving things out. In addressing Henry James on *Treasure Island*, he says that "the characters are portrayed only so far as they realize the sense of danger and provoke the sympathy of fear. To add more traits, to be too clever, to start the hare of moral or intellectual interest while we are running the fox of material interest, is not to enrich but to stultify your tale."

Like Edgar Allen Poe in his essays on poetry, Stevenson is here describing his own practice and accounting for his own work more than he is analyzing the nature of romance; but the distinction he makes, vital to what counts for him in writing, is illuminating from a working writer's point of view. The writers of realistic fiction—the kind Henry James was in the process of creating, or re-creating, the kind most writers write now—spend much of their efforts trying to *add meaning* to the things in their stories, by various writerly means, usually while trying to conceal their efforts from the reader. The old house is not, for the characters and therefore for the readers, simply an old house; the inheritance is more than just an inheritance; the car more than a car. Of course it is. Virginia Woolf's lighthouse, or her moths. The Joad's truck in *The Grapes of Wrath* or the coffin in *As I Lay Dying*. What Stevenson says is that in novels of adventure, in romance—at least in the kind he conceives—the things don't require this added meaning, in fact can't use it; they must *be,* simply and cleanly, what they are; the pieces of gold are simply glittering and desirable, the ship is only tall and swift and imperiled. And of course this is right too. But if a writer is unable to create things and places and moments with the authority of a Stevenson, can't grant them the living brilliance, the transparency, that Stevenson can, then the fact of their having been given no added meaning by the writer will often mean that they have no life whatever; they lose actuality and have only a factitious activeness, like the things and people in a computer game—computer games being, in fact, the terminus of one branch of the adventure tale in our time.

The computer game, the genre fantasy novel, the Marvel comic, all aim at and even share a certain—shall we call it an audience?—and it is one central to Stevenson's conception of his writing and even of himself as a writer. A well-known science fiction writer, when asked about the Golden Age of science fiction, replied that the Golden Age of science fiction is twelve. And we are to understand by this—though less now perhaps than at one time—twelve-year-old *boys*. Girls have their own genres.

In writing *Treasure Island*, Stevenson said to James, he was consciously writing a boy's book for grownups: He no more than James had ever gone questing after gold, but he was, he says, "well aware (cunning and low-minded man!) that this class of interest, having been frequently treated, finds a readily accessible and beaten road to the sympathies of the reader," and he "addressed himself throughout to the building up and circumstantiation of this boyish dream." Stevenson justifies his bold reductive swiftness because it is thus that successful boys' adventures must be written.

Now it has been pointed out by Leslie Fiedler that the central fictions of the American canon, from Cooper's novels through *Moby-Dick* to *Huckleberry Finn*, have all spent time on the children's shelf of the library, as books for boys. (Books that fail to make this grade, Fiedler opines, can end up, like Thomas Wolfe's novels, as books for adolescents.) A distinction ought to be made, though: those books, which do not by any means all meet Stevenson's criteria of swiftness and simplicity, were all written for adults; whereas Stevenson is quite conscious not only of himself as boy, participating in the creation of and appreciating the unfolding of his own inventions, but of the actual audience of boys who he suspects will read the finished books. But writing for boys, like cooking for boys, depends for success more on quantity and familiarity than on quality. Did Stevenson wonder, finally, whether the effort it took to bring off such astonishing things as, for instance, the Hispaniola's journey adrift around Treasure Island, was in fact unnecessary? Would he have recognized, if he could have seen them, that the Classic Comics version of *Kidnapped*, or the Disney version of *Treasure Island*, actually contained all the magnetic essence of those works, and that his additional labor over them was largely wasted? He forgives Walter Scott for being so often slack and witless and inattentive because Scott has the right romance stuff; did he ever wonder whether the fact that he himself evidently had the right romance stuff meant that, whatever airs he gave himself, or Henry James gave him, what was finally interesting to readers about his works was not what he thought special to them—what he prized in them—but what they shared with a large class of fictions? *There must be something wrong with me, if I am popular.* Was he himself at bottom a sort of Scott? Doesn't it seem likely that, much as he professed to love Scott, he would have hated the idea?

There is of course another, or obverse, side of the dilemma I have described (dilemmas having two at a minimum). It's not only that Stevenson's personal standards and strengths were in a sense irrelevant to the production of effective adventure stories; it is that they actually *were* necessary if Stevenson were to try to free himself from the apparent bottomless childhood freedom of the adventure tale and write those other stories, or limn those other circumstances, that he also deeply felt; that were not common property, but his alone.

The critic John Bayley has noted that a great novel inevitably creates an elsewhere. The sugar at the ball supper in *Madame Bovary* is whiter than the sugar in our world. Vladimir Nabokov says that the great novels of the realist tradition are actually great fairy tales. Stevenson was thinking along these lines in likening a work of art to a proposition in geometry: "both inhere in nature, neither represents it." A work of art, he says, is "neat, self-contained, rational, flowing and emasculate." And though he does not explicitly say so, it seems that he thinks of the romance, specifically the boy's adventure tale, as the ideal case of this in narrative fiction. It isn't; rather it's the *trompe-l'oeil* novel that baffles the reader into thinking, for a moment, that it really is like life, just as bright, just as poignant, just as monstrous: only to dissolve, at a subtle wave of the writer's wand, into words—into the face of the writer, cruel or kind or godlike and grave.

And how is *that* trick done?

What Stevenson was discovering, or what lay ahead of him to be discovered, was that there is finally no difference between how a writer, a Stevenson, gives life, vividness, transparency to the exigencies of an adventure novel, and how that writer will illuminate, make wonderful and strange, any sort of event or encounter; and when a writer who has sought for wonder and captivation in the exotic or the drastic finds that he can transform, redeem, the diurnal and even the autobiographical *by exactly the same means*, not more timidly but actually more ruthlessly applied—there's a new joy in the discovery, a joy that in itself powers the work of transformation. It's the joy, the ease we can feel (strangely enough, but it's there) in the death of the mother in *Weir of Hermiston*—the right sort of thing falling out in the right sort of way, the threads of the story coming together to form a picture in the web, a character falling into an attitude which stamps the story like an illustration.

Can we think of Stevenson in the last year or two of his life, that time of wonderful enthusiasm and strength, coming to a new sense of just how far his gifts could reach? That to do what he wanted to do in fiction did not in fact mean depending on the standard units of adventure and romance fiction, that it was all in fact up to him, and he could do as he liked? What *did* he like? At the end of his life he was still turning over those romantic circumstances that were obviously always going to be connected with the deepest wells of his creativity—the Covenanters gathering, the hills of home, the old wayside tavern. The work he was doing, though, seemed to be mutating, not always easily or evenly, into something with the force and simplicity of his adventure writing, but with its heart in another place.

It must be acknowledged, at the last, that the dilemma very often—always?—makes the writer. In early stories—*The New Arabian Nights*, *The Pavilion on the Links*—the characters' longing to find themselves in a romance, their delight in finding or believing themselves to be in one, mirror the readers' and the writer's own delight and gratification; in *Kidnapped* and *Treasure Island* there is not this self-consciousness about romance, and no uncertainty either. But the difficulties Stevenson had with *The Master of Ballantrae* were due it seems to me to Stevenson's assumption that the working out of a romance plot was easier than it is, particularly for him, and perhaps to doubts about whether the work was worth doing well. People read it anyway, in numbers. Down to the last projected books, Stevenson and his dear public were engaged in an embrace sometimes indistinguishable from an agon.

What the present has to envy in Stevenson is the fluidity of the relation that still obtained between genre writer and consuming public, that allowed for the working out of a destiny rather than the mere treading of a path. It may well be that in even the most restricted genres being written today—in horror novels and sword-and-sorcery tales, books read only by their target readership—beauty and the privileged moments Stevenson writes of are being created, and by Stevenson's means, that is, exquisite care for language and knowledge of the heart's desire. Such writing will last its two weeks on the shelves along with the rest, in covers indistinguishable from its fellows, and will be praised by fans in terms also indistinguishable from the praise bestowed on others. Then it will be pulped or its acidic paper will destroy itself; and long before then it will have been swept aside by a host of others like it in most respects except that they are not good—dim, slack, knotless—and it is. A Dark Ages it seems can be brought about as easily by too many books as too few. Writers today who share Stevenson's secret springs, and believe they may share at least some of his gifts, cannot make Stevenson's blithe assumption that they will be able to use them in the creation of romances, and still have their work recognized as good, not simply good of its kind. Maybe it will be; maybe not.

Finally I will put in evidence a new book, currently in bound galleys, that would have confirmed the worst fears that I have imputed to or projected onto Robert Louis Stevenson. Here is *Treasure Island*, a new novel by Justin Scott. And here are the opening paragraphs:

> Senator Trelawney and Dr. Livesey have asked me to write everything that happened on Treasure Island—except its actual coordinates, because we left a ton of loot behind. Start to finish, the Senator demands. The whole blood-stained story.
> So I go back to the 1950s, just before my father died. Back when doctors smoked and men were supposed to "watch their language" in front of kids; back when Mom said "the war" she meant World War Two [sic]; back when we owned a rundown restaurant-tourist home on the Great South Bay called the Admiral Benbow Hotel.

It's like that all the way through, very nearly paragraph for paragraph, *mutatis* just barely *mutandis*. The loot is Nazi gold lost by a deserted submarine. Squire Trelawney has become a blustering U.S. senator. Dr. Livesey is the same firm and competent figure—well, almost:

> "One more thing," continued the doctor. "I'll be watching for you. I'm a medical examiner as well as a doctor. Every cop and state trooper in Suffolk County knows I can do him a favor. If I hear one word about you causing trouble I'll make you wish you never heard of Long Island." With

that, she stalked out, flinging her wool cape over her shoulders, fired up her Jeep, and splashed into the night.

This is not a joke, or a pastiche; it is not a post-modern *jeu d'esprit*, like Borges's *Pierre Menard, Author of the Quixote*. It is simply an attempt to get a good adventure story to a wider public: a fate whose logic Stevenson himself in hell might appreciate, but which he could not perhaps have imagined. That was left to the book packagers of the present moment.

1994

ROBERT LOUIS STEVENSON by Frank McLynn and THE LETTERS OF ROBERT LOUIS STEVENSON, Volumes III and IV, edited by Ernest Mehew

If we who are not experts wish to know the lives of men and women who have touched us by their works, we are for the most part at the mercy of professional biographers. We listen to them avidly, like bedridden aunts listening to news of family members whom they cannot visit for themselves; we try to assess their tales and their conclusions by watching for whatever bias we can discern in their statements about matters we are familiar with, or have our own opinions on; we match what they tell us with the person we imagine we know from the works. We reject what seems to us wrong, or what we don't want to hear.

This year is the centenary of the death of Robert Louis Stevenson, and a new biography (there have been many) by Frank McLynn now appears here; it came out in Britain to considerable notice last year. Stevenson is one of those writers—like Jack London and Ernest Hemingway and Lord Byron—whose lives bear an ambiguous but never ignorable relation to their authorship: every writer's life does, of course, but there are writers whose stance or adventure in life seems to belong among their own works, in a different medium but similar in ambition. Stevenson—the sickly boy who longed for adventure, and who really did sail away at last to tropic isles, never to return; Stevenson, who at different times thought that the making of art was the reason for his life, and at other times that the greatest art was inferior to a great gesture, a romantic act, and who actually did make gestures and act acts that admirers have been able to interpret as great and romantic, though he might not himself have—Stevenson is as good as his books, and the problem for the biographers has been to disentangle them.

There are several cruces that have been much worked over: his Scots Calvinism, and its effects on the life, and on the work; his lifelong illness—it is not even certain what it was; and his popularity: was he, finally, a lightweight? Has he been underrated? Overrated?

And there is Fanny.

All biographers of Stevenson are bound to take some stance toward Fanny Osbourne. She was an American, a Hoosier, veteran of the Western mining camps, whom Stevenson met in France when he was 26 and she 36. She was married, to a philandering knockabout back in California, and had two children (a third had just died of a long and painful illness when Stevenson met her). The family legend was that he fell in love with her at first sight; this isn't likely, but I have always supposed that she was the first woman he both loved and slept with, and McLynn has no hard evidence that I'm wrong. What is certain is that he gave unstintingly of himself to her and her children, made a journey from Scotland to California to be with her when she called to him, a journey that nearly killed him; and that he lived all his life with her in situations, from ocean crossings on small boats to jungle homesteading, that would try the soundest of marriages.

Was Fanny also a tyrannizing and selfish hypochondriac who drained Stevenson of his resources (financial and otherwise) in favor of herself and her brood, who deliberately alienated his friends in order to have him for herself, who kept him (out of pride or greed) from writing the best work he could, and who on one occasion actually forced him to destroy it? This is what we hear (hands cupped behind our ears and heads ashake) from Frank McLynn.

McLynn feels that he is duty-bound to counteract a conspiracy of "mythmakers" who have distorted the record in order to present Fanny as a devoted nurse and helpmeet, and foolish biographers who have been duped by Fanny and her family into believing that Stevenson cherished them, and they him. His animus against Fanny and her son Lloyd and daughter Belle (Stevenson called them his family, and Lloyd his son; to McLynn they are always "the

Osbournes") is apparent on every page where they appear, in big matters as in small, and deepens as he carries them forward.

"A very rum creature indeed," he calls her early on; "those who persist in presenting the relationship of RLS and Fanny as a storybook love story have a lot of explaining to do" at one point; in California "her description of Louis's near-fatal illness cannot be described as anything other than flip and cavalier"; when they acquire a dog, "Fanny [!] could not be bothered to house-train it, so it left a trail of faeces all over French hotels"; Fanny is not a passionate or a hardworking gardener but a "fanatic" one; arguments flare because of "the tensions between the nest-building, comfort-seeking, aspiring bourgeois, her eye always on the commercial marketplace, and the restless, driven Magian rover whose commitment to his art was, as he admitted, greater than that to wife and adopted family." These are nearly random selections; I have more.

Is this justified? How is a non-expert to know? When we listen to gossip that is continually to the gossipee's discredit, we cease to entirely trust the gossiper. McLynn's loathing (there is really no other word) causes us to recast his interpretations into their opposites, just to see they make as good sense that way (often as not they do). We watch to see if the hated object is damned if she does as well as if she doesn't, and surely Fanny is: that nest-building comfort-seeking bourgeois is the same tough independent woman who squatted with Louis in a Silverado miner's cabin on their honeymoon, and who suggested the Pacific adventure from which neither ever returned to bourgeois comforts.

We also check our own responses to incidents where enough evidence is given to allow us to judge. "Fanny's much-vaunted nursing skills (as in the Fanny legend) had left her husband unimpressed," McLynn says, and as evidence gives this letter of Stevenson to Fanny:

> I don't want you when I am ill. At least it's only half of me that wants you, and I don't like to think of your coming back and not finding me better than when we parted. That is why I should rather be miserable than send for you.

Now does this actually deeply touching letter bear the interpretation put on it? Don't most sick people—those with as sharp a sense of *amour-propre* as Stevenson's—hate to have those they love most see them weak and needy, and isn't that what Stevenson meant?

Instances of this sort of callous misreading can again be multiplied; they multiply as the reader grows more critical, and begins to wonder about the many assertions for which no evidence at all is given. There is for instance the matter of the first draft of *Dr. Jekyll and Mr. Hyde*.

It is a famous moment in Stevenson biography. Stevenson has just finished the first draft of a new kind of story, the horrid premises of which came to him in dreams; he has written at white heat, possibly 8,000 words a day. Fanny reads the draft, and is very hard on it; there is a long and loud discussion; and Stevenson throws the draft into the fire. He immediately begins on a second draft, completes it almost as fast, and it makes him famous.

McLynn asks: "Why did Stevenson destroy a manuscript which was . . . 'the best thing he had ever done;' why did he ever afterwards assert that *Jekyll* was a negligible achievement, because Fanny had ruined the version he wanted to publish?" The answer he gives to his own already tendentious questions is that Fanny wanted commercial success, and that the draft she read dealt too frankly with sex, and would destroy his career as a writer of children's adventure stories.

The draft is burned, and no one can read it. It seems neither Fanny nor Stevenson ever said what it was about the draft that Fanny objected to. Did Stevenson really say seriously that the book was negligible because Fanny had ruined the version he wanted to publish? McLynn quotes no letters. We can only judge by who we think these people are: and in my judgment it isn't possible that Stevenson would destroy superior work and replace it with inferior because of anybody's judgment; nor can I think Fanny would want him to. I bet (I have no documentary evidence to offer) that the argument was about matters Stevenson was always weakest in: plot, structure, and the management of the moral ambiguities he was so drawn to. Criticism of a writer's genuine weaknesses, especially the ones he consistently indulges, are the most hurtful.

Shall we turn then, in doubt, to other experts? Which ones, exactly? When McLynn's book appeared in Britain it was warmly praised by many, including Anthony Burgess, though some reviewers puzzled over his obvious Fanny vendetta. In the *Times Literary Supplement* the book was reviewed by Ernest Mehew, who took issue with much of the interpretation. This started one of those nasty squabbles in the letters column that the British conduct with such relish. McLynn in his own defense complained that "amateur experts" like Mehew "are the bane of the serious writer."

Ernest Mehew is in fact the editor of a new and huge edition of Stevenson's letters, on which he has been at work for many years, and which is coming out in several volumes from Yale University Press. The third and fourth volumes are just now appearing, and are as scrupulously and fairly finished as the previous ones—an edition as well done as one could wish, for a letter-writer who belongs with the greatest in English, alongside (my own choice of companions) Virginia Woolf and Byron.

This is the amateur expert who plagues serious writer McLynn, author of a handful of biographies and histories on largely non-literary topics. Mehew says McLynn is simply wrong on the facts; McLynn says Mehew simply cannot embrace his new interpretation: "Admirers of a totally fictitious RLS, such as Mehew, in effect play down his heroism and courage [in putting up with the Osbournes] and thus turn him into a one-dimensional uxorious buffoon."

Each to his own. For me, it is McLynn's Stevenson who is one-dimensional, and a uxorious buffoon too if he could not see through so transparent a villainess as McLynn's Fanny. Fanny has always seemed to me above all American, and I think it was a genuineness and an openness, an unwillingness to adopt social masks, that was the most attractive thing about her to Stevenson, and the most off-putting to his British acquaintances. It may be what made her sometimes difficult to live with, too. Henry James called her a "poor, barbarous and merely *instinctive* lady," which was perhaps right from a Jamesian point of view; Henry's sister Alice noted "such egotism and so naked! giving me the strangest feeling of being in the presence of an unclothed being," not a good thing obviously, but maybe also right in its way.

McLynn quotes Alice's remark twice, with evident approval; he admits that Henry got along pretty well with Fanny, but says that "perhaps as an American, used to matriarchy, he had an instinctive understanding of the type of woman Fanny was."

Maybe it's just an American, or matriarchal, thing: McLynn finally seems to me to have no understanding of the type of woman

Fanny was. On the other hand he is unable to convince this reader that he understands the sort of person Robert Louis Stevenson was either, or why his books are worth reading. His ubiquitous Freudian categories are blunt instruments which he wields with a judgmental, not to say punitive, lack of sympathy. I found his literary analyses jejune, and learned nothing that I hoped to learn about the making, publishing and selling of popular literature and the earning of royalties in the late nineteenth century. Just as family gossip, though we long to hear it, often tells us more about the teller than the told-about, we get in this book deeper and richer glimpses into the unique soul of the biographer than we ever get into his subject. As a memorial to Stevenson in his centenary year, and a reminder of his stature, both literary and personal, I will stay with Mehew's letters.

1994

MARY REILLY by Valerie Martin

It has been noted that Robert Louis Stevenson's *Dr. Jekyll and Mr Hyde* is as empty of female presences as a London club. The lawyer Utterson and the young businessmen Enfield who between them tell the story, Dr. Jekyll himself, even the butler Poole, are all bachelors. Hyde's sins may involve women, but unlike Oscar Wilde in *The Picture of Dorian Gray*, Stevenson forbore to name them or to describe them except in horrid generalities.

Now Valerie Martin has had the terrific idea of retelling the story of Dr. Jekyll and Mr. Hyde from the point of view of someone who might well have been a witness to the events, but who was invisible to the original tellers—doubly invisible, for Mary Reilly is not only a woman but a servant. The idea is such a natural that as soon as the reader gets it he seems almost to have thought it up himself, and to be able to imagine in delight all that will follow. It is to Valerie Martin's credit that what does follow is never quite predictable.

Stevenson's story, like Mary Shelley's story of Frankenstein and the stories of Sherlock Holmes, has come to belong not to its author but to all of us, a fable of emerging scientific rationalism as necessary to our moral education as Prometheus or Pygmalion once were. That by chemical treatment we can precipitate out the evil nature within our ordinary law-abiding well-meaning natures, and thus perhaps rid ourselves of it; that in attempting to do so a heroic overreaching scientist becomes not free of but enslaved to his own worser self—if Stevenson had not first distilled the story, someone else would have had to.

Valerie Martin's Mary Reilly, housemaid in Dr. Jekyll's well-run London house, is not drawn to the oppositions that tempt and destroy her Master (as she always names him). She has suffered from uncontrolled demonic sadism—her father, through the agency of no more sophisticated a chemical than gin, tortured her unforgivably when she was a child, and she doesn't forgive, nor forget: but she has a sense of the unalterability of what is, and the strength to find a way to live and even to love despite it. Unable to grasp the cause, she can still experience vividly the human cost of Jekyll's experiment.

Martin's greatest triumph in her sidelong retelling is how convincing she makes Mary Reilly and her life belowstairs. The novel is told in the first person; Mary Reilly has been given a little education at a school in which Dr. Jekyll once took a philanthropic interest (Mary doesn't tell him how poor a place it was) and she fills her penny notebooks late at night while the house is asleep. Her voice, without being pedantically authentic, is entirely genuine. She is trying to make an herb garden in the dark yard that separates the comfortable house from the dark laboratory:

"I set to work with Cook's direction, and heavy work it was, as the ground was so hard it come up in great clods. Cook said first those ugly bushes mun go and they gave me a fair struggle, though they hardly looked alive, and I thought how all plants do struggle and seem to be longing to flourish no matter how badly they are treated or on what hard, unprofitable soil they fall, so I began to feel a little sorry for the poor bushes, but Cook said they'd be the death of our herbs so up they mun come." (Mary already feels the difficulty involved in weeding out the strong evil to let the delicate good flourish. It takes great and delicate art to allow so stark a symbol to spring up in a book, and to have it do work, without seeming to have been planted: Stevenson was himself a master of it.)

Mary is committed to service, in all of its meanings; she is as loyal to her house and as proud of it, as acutely concerned for its honor, as a junior officer in a crack regiment. She is clear-eyed about her position, and her prospects, but never bitter; she is largely unnoticed by upstairs, but though they exclude her, she includes them, and sees them more clearly than they see themselves. The only person who sees as clearly as she does is Mr. Edward Hyde.

The story seen from the servants' hall is of a natural order overturned. Dr. Jekyll is a good man and a good master; his house is well run and stable, as many houses are not. The first sign of trouble is that the master on whom they all depend, whose wellbeing they all identify with their own, seems intent on ruining his health with poor diet, late nights, and overwork. They sense but cannot formulate the connection between this weakness of their master's and the sudden parasitic appearance of Edward Hyde, whom the servants are shocked to learn has been given "the freedom of the house." Hyde's worst characteristic, as they see it, is that though he pretends to authority, he is *not a gentleman:* Jekyll's subjection to him is a breach in nature.

Martin abjures the most lurid temptations her scheme might have suggested to her. Mary Reilly's contacts with her Master and his other are few; her life is filled not with drama but with work—cleaning grates, hauling coal, beating carpets and draperies, helping Cook. Every slight advance in intimacy she makes with Dr. Jekyll, every brief glimpse she has of the wrongness at the household's heart, she hoards up to wring its meaning out. The narrowness of her view of Jekyll and his danger is overcome by the intensity of her vision. Her straightforward human concern for her troubled Master he answers with distracted gestures of casual kindness, but they are enough for Mary: her concern transmutes to a love willing to risk anything, yet still not strong enough to save him.

The greatest artistic difficulty Martin faces is one she has inherited from her original. We often forget that *Dr. Jekyll and Mr. Hyde* is a mystery story: Only in the last pages do we learn the secret of Jekyll's relation to Hyde. Even in the original the mystery is not well sustained, and is now obviated for every reader; the *longeurs* in *Mary Reilly* are all due to what we know and Mary tries fruitlessly to discover. Conversely, the most genuinely suspenseful moments (and the strongest writing) come when the terrible father whom Mary long ago escaped is glimpsed again, and may appear before her, like a Hyde of her own: and we don't know what will happen.

Mary Reilly is an achievement, creativity skating exhilaratingly on thin ice. It shares with some of Valerie Martin's earlier work (along with an apparent obsession with rats) a compulsion to bring together ordinary people with others who are wholly good (as in *A Recent Martyr*) or wholly evil. The radical indefinability of the key terms suggests a difficulty with such a schema, and it's a difficulty in *Mary Reilly*'s original as well. I think Valerie Martin's treatment of the story actually succeeds in ways that Stevenson himself could not have brought off, and might well have admired.

1990

~ THOMAS M. DISCH ~

THE LIST OF THOMAS M. DISCH'S published works just inside his latest novel is printed in small type, and even so threatens to run onto a second page. There are twelve novels, five collections of short fiction, several books of poetry, a classic children's story (*The Brave Little Toaster*) and its sequel. There are plays, including an adaptation of *Ben Hur*, opera libretti, and a work of interactive software called *Amnesia*. Coming last in the list of plays is *The Cardinal Detoxes*, a one-act play in blank verse, which got its author and producing company in trouble with the Archdiocese of New York—the landlord, as it happened, of the theater where the play was running. The archdiocese's efforts to evict the company no doubt brought Disch visions of the *Index librorum prohibitorum* and a thrilling whiff of the *auto-da-fé*.

The Archbishop of New York appears on the dedication page of his new novel, along with Father Bruce Ritter, Father James Porter, the Servants of the Paraclete in Jemez Springs, New Mexico, and His Holiness, Pope John Paul II, "without whose ministry and conjoint power of example this novel could not have been written."[†] The novel is titled *The Priest: A Gothic Romance*.

The most famous of all Gothic romances was called *The Monk* (1796), and enjoyed vast success in England and America in part because the Catholic Church, its fabled power, occult processes, dramatic accoutrements, big architecture, and supposed implacable zeal were so vivid and shudder-starting to white-church Protestants and rationalists. Matthew Gregory Lewis, who came to be called "Monk" Lewis for his most famous book, altered the milder

---

[†] The dedication was actually removed from the American edition; I read the British edition. [Author's note]

Gothic-novel tradition of Walpole and Ann Radcliffe, adding actual supernatural events to their apparent ones, and loads of desperate compulsive sex, including an affair between a priest and a novice (a girl in disguise, but the point is taken).

The Priest comes at the end of the Lewis tradition; it is set in contemporary Minneapolis, amid declining congregations, multiplying sex scandals, and anti-abortion demonstrations, but it offers most of the thrills of its great predecessor, along with the tang of contemporary relevance and a species of dreadful hilarity that the Church and its doings can often inspire in her lost or banished children.

Disch also once wrote, under the imposing pseudonym of "Leonie Hargreave," a Gothic of the other sort, the kind where all the fearful possibilities resolve themselves as mere human extravagance and wickedness; it was called *Clara Reeve*, its heroine named after another of the ancestral Gothic novelists. His opera libretti include adaptations of *The Fall of the House of Usher* and *Frankenstein*. So the Gothic is a familiar métier, but there is hardly a narrative form Disch has not tried, and stretched, and reshaped. His early novels were science fiction, a form to which many questing and restless talents were drawn in the 1960s; the most unlikely books could in those years be published as science fiction and sell copies, and set a young writer out (perhaps over-optimistically) on a career. (*Ice*, a heroin-induced rhapsody by the English recluse Anna Kavan, appeared in the U.S. in those years as an sf paperback.) The name "science fiction" is actually a masking term for a whole range of fictions which can share certain superficial resemblances but actually belong to different genres—Gothic, philosophical romance, utopian speculation, boys' adventure (pirate or cowboy story), modern dread, postmodern whimsy. A couple of Disch's sf novels (*The Puppies of Terra*, *Camp Concentration*) are describable as philosophical romances, but the most characteristic of them—*334*, *On Wings of Song*—are unlike any others in the field. Most writing about the future is purposeful: it intends some sort of warning, or promise, or encouragement or discouragement; some sort of moral. These futures of Disch's have moral intensity but no single moral direction; they are permeated with a kind of melancholy reflection, they possess the randomness, the knowable and yet unsummable multiplicity, the poignancy that we associate with the past, and writing about the past. These futures bring in hard things, and new species of oppression; but they bring in new possibilities, too, which souls rise to or fail to rise to. They are like life, which is the one thing most sf is not like.

Ambition in genre writing is often a perilous thing. The undiscriminating taste of genre readers—actually a highly discriminating taste, but a taste which discriminates only its kind of book from all others, aesthetic quality aside—and the invisibility of genre writing to all other readers, are only aspects of the problem. There is centrally the question of whether the forms and constraints of any of the modern genres—horror, say, or sf, or "romance," or sword-and-sorcery, or the Western—are worth struggling with, worth the effort of transforming. What readership will witness your labors, or be able to understand what you have done?

Beginning with *The Businessman* (1984) Thomas M. Disch has been creating a series of novels that are at once comprehensible within a genre and have aesthetic and perhaps other ambitions well beyond the usual scope of such books. *The Businessman* is subtitled "A Tale of Terror"; *The M.D.*, second in the series, is subtitled "A Horror Story," and the latest, *The Priest,* as noted, is "A Gothic Romance." None of these subtitles is exactly accurate, but the writer is playing fair with his most likely readers: these are not pastiches, parodies, or postmodern japes. They are published by the very literary house of Alfred A. Knopf, but they also bear blurbs from Stephen King. The delicacy of the literary problem Disch has set himself, to say nothing of the complex career choice, are often present to the reader's mind: to this reader's, at any rate.

All three books are set in Minneapolis in approximately the present day (*The M.D* reaches a few years into the future). A few characters play parts in more than one book, and there are places in the city important in all three, but they are unconnected in plot. More importantly, within each a different kind of spiritual or supernatural realm envelops the city, not mutually exclusive but particular to each book, a part of its individual *geist* as the characters and the flavor of the language are.

The Businessman is a ghost story. The central characters are mostly dead, and learning to live with it. Alive almost to the end is the marvelously-named Bob Glandier, businessman and self-indulgent moral wreck, who has murdered his wife Giselle in a rage after discovering her in a Las Vegas motel room (Las Vegas is the distant capital city of Disch's world here) where she has fled from him. Her afterlife will consist for a time in the unpleasant job of haunting him, a thing she has no real say about. At first, in the grave, she knows nothing at all:

> Her body was here in the coffin *with* her, and in some way she was still linked to its disintegrating proteins, but it wasn't through her body's senses that she knew these things. There was only this suspended sphere of self-awareness beyond which she could discern certain dim essentials of the earth immuring her—a dense, moist, intricate mass pierced with constellations of forward-inching hungers, nodules of intensity against a milky radiance of calm bacterial transformation.
>
> *The worms crawl in*—she remembered the rhyme from childhood. *The worms crawl out. The worms play pinochle on your snout.*

Giselle, her dead mother Joy-Ann, and the spirits of Adah Isaacs Menken and the poet John Berryman (who committed suicide by jumping from a well-known bridge in Minneapolis, and whose ghost still resides unreleased beneath it, looking horribly shattered and bloody but in no pain except for needing a drink) combine not very purposefully but in the end effectively to fix Bob Glandier's wagon, and thus permit Giselle to move up a stage in the afterlife, which is a complex place but full of interest, its interaction with our lives on earth reasonable and explicable, though not predictable, even from the other side.

The Businessman resembles other ghost stories less than it does those rare and deeply gratifying Hollywood fantasies, films like *Here Comes Mr. Jordan* or *It's a Wonderful Life*, where the writers have worked out in detail wholly original but wonderfully supple and consistent spiritual worlds and their earthly consequences. In Disch's book the glamour and repletion provided in the movies by the presence of star actors and the glow of masterly cinematography are supplied by the narrator's voice—a voice of marvelous grave gaiety, offering pleasures generously but modestly, making no judgments it has not already led the reader into making, and awarding to the characters joys and punishments that are equally gratifying to hear about. Only lengthy quotation could show how, sentence to sentence, this is accomplished; best to read the whole. The reader is reminded, very strangely, of Disch's fellow Minnesotan Sinclair Lewis, and of *Babbitt* in particular: the joyful care with which Lewis describes the contents of George Babbitt's bathroom cabinet, or the choosing of his suit; how while seeming to be engaged in excoriating provincial errors of taste and moral inadequacy he communicates such relish for the details of the places and lives he displays, such love even, that the reader feels his smile, and is warmed by it. It is a very strange tone to be taking in a horror novel, and the success of it adds to the exhilaration.

The M.D., next in the series, is a different matter; not only darker in coloration, but different in how the supernatural interacts with life on earth. Billy Michaels, growing up in Minneapolis and attending Our Lady of Mercy School, has a vision of Santa Claus, and has a vivid if ambiguous conversation with him. Sister Symphorosa, his teacher, has told him that Santa is like a pagan god, and doesn't exist; she is right in the first claim, wrong in the second. Santa—who has chosen to appear to Billy Michaels in exactly the arbitrary way that gods were once said to visit men—is in fact a manifestation of the god Mercury, patron of medicine, and of liars. He has a gift for Billy, and an exaction to make in return. The gift is a sort of caduceus, with which Billy will be able to both make certain people sick and make others well: the exaction is a lifelong bondage to the god. Billy will find that his caduceus can only retain its power to heal if it is periodically recharged by being used to do harm; he can't imagine, at ten years old, all that this will mean—how much harm he will find himself capable of—and the working-out of this awful destiny, as in a Greek tragedy (or a Senecan one), will issue at length in madness, degradation, and parricide.

There is a difficulty here, and it has to do with the fantastic in literature in it widest application. In realistic novels—the sort that comprises not only most of what fill the front of the bookstores but most crime, spy and mystery novels as well—the mythemes out of older literature are deployed as metaphor, to give a layer of added meaning to the events and dilemmas of the story. The hints of damnation, magic, the selling of the soul for power, are used in this way in Mann's *Dr. Faustus*. In other genres, though—I almost wrote "the lesser genres"—the supernatural or magical dimension is simply there, posited, a problem and a possibility for the characters. Billy Michaels is visited by a god; in exchange for the power the god has in his favor to bestow, Billy gives him what all gods want: worship and commitment. Taking place as they do in a realistic, even hyper-realistic setting, in a novel that is in every other way in the familiar vein of common realism, these things may seem problematic; they are radically unproblematic. They do not *stand for* the corruptions of power, or the temptations of imperial science, or the end not justifying the means; they are what they are. We are in a fairy tale; Billy's wishes will come true, and we will see what a boy like this, in this world of ours, will do with them.

This genre effect permeates the book, shifting conversations, events, and crises continuously away from what the same things would mean in a book of a different kind. Here is Billy talking to his beloved anoretic stepsister:

> "So, have you ever *prayed* to be cured?"
> "Prayer isn't like that, William," she protested. "It's not like going to the Santa at Dayton's and giving him a list of what you want for Christmas. It's a conversation, like we're having, only it's God we're talking with."
> "If you needed something from me that I could give you, you'd ask me for it, wouldn't you? . . ."

God, in Disch's world, may be unable to answer prayers; but her brother can, and will.

The M.D. is a fairy tale, but it is also a long, circumstantial, realistic novel. Minneapolis, a Catholic childhood, Billy's shifting family relations, are gravely and fully drawn. Billy Michaels has an obdurate opacity despite our being allowed to understand him by most of the usual novelistic means; his absorption in his power, learning to understand and use it, seems to drain away his ordinariness, without in any way enlarging him: it leaves, in the end, nothing behind, an awful vacuity. And perhaps such power would do just that.

This would be a fine novel even with a different sort of engine in it; the magical, or demonic—which grows in power and dreadfulness as the book reaches into the future—continually unbalances and challenges the reader, always forcing further attention, an exaction not every reader will be comfortable with. But the tension is wonderfully maintained, and it is not always easy to see how this is done; the narrative voice forgoes the obvious delight in people and things everywhere felt in *The Businessman*, and gives less guidance, though it can be often equally fine in its effects. Billy's mother playing Frisbee with her son in a rare moment of easy connection with the doomed boy:

> It was wonderful all the different flight paths you could make it trace. She had no idea what twist of wrist or flick of the fingers made it follow one trajectory instead of another. It was all done unconsciously but with a strange precision. You'd almost think the plastic disk had a volition and intelligence of its own, as though it were some species of bird that had been fined down to this bare anatomical minimum, a living discus skimming the lowest branches of the maple, whirling toward the patio and then veering away, settling down on the mown grass with a whoosh of deceleration like a waterfowl coming to rest on a lake.

Eventually the book must cease to vary its forward rush with such moments; there is much bloody work to be done, and we know it, for we are, after all, reading a horror novel, and like pornographic novels horror novels must make their particular effects keep coming a little more quickly, each a little more replete than the last. Which makes the cool poignancy of this momentary aerial suspension the more gratifying. This is a profoundly original book, whose originality is all the more puzzling in a genre where originality is rare.

The Priest is, again, a different kettle of fish. The reader may suppose—Disch gives some reason to think it—that *The M.D.* is an indictment of the corruptions of power; I think this is a minor aspect. But *The Priest* is an outright philippic on the subject, with immediate reference to the daily papers. Here is another new use of the horror genre, which is again likely to be unsettling to fans and non-consumers alike.

The earthly world of *The Priest* can be triangulated on three churches: there is Our Lady of Mercy downtown; newer and sleeker St. Bernardine's in the upscale suburb of Willowville; and the huge completed but unused shrine, Speer-like and granitic, of Blessed Konrad of Paderborn, built up north on the shores of Leech Lake near Etoile du Nord Seminary (I assumed Disch had made up these place-names; a map tells me they are quite real). Blessed Konrad, star of a medieval anti-Semitic martyr legend, has had approval of his cult withdrawn by Rome in the wake of protests; but the shrine, overseen by fanatic Gerhardt Ober and his sister Hedwig, is being used for other purposes.

Pastor of St. Bernardine's, late of OLM, is Father Pat Bryce, not a pedophile (as he learns) but an ephebophile, who has often begun the seduction of his lads while in the darkness of the confessional:

> There was nothing that so transfixed him as hearing the voice of a boy who had never come to confession to him before haltingly explaining that he had been guilty of sins of the flesh. What sins *exactly*, he would have to know, how many times, and where, and what acts had the boy *imagined* as he masturbated? . . . For Father Bryce the moment of release was the moment he could feel a boy's will yielding to his. It was not necessarily a carnal moment, though carnality might well be the end result.
>
> It was, however, always a *priestly* moment, for a priest is a bender and shaper of wills.

Father Pat, who is to be himself bent and shaped, is at St. Bernardine's because of his tastes. When a boy lover in psychological trouble spills the beans, the scandal is hushed up; Father Pat is sent to a clinic in Arizona (where like ordinary hoods and criminals he learns lots of new tricks from fellow inmates) and then given a new assignment by the hierarchy, which he is in no position to refuse: from his new post at St. Bernardine's he is to be operator of a new and radical, as yet wholly secret, passing move in the Church's anti-abortion campaign. Parents of pregnant teenagers are to be convinced to sign over their girls to the Church authorities, who by force if necessary will keep them sequestered in the basements of the derelict shrine of Blessed Konrad of Paderborn (built to be nuclear bomb-proof,) cared for by the Obers until their children are born. The Church will thus be able to communicate to her shock troops in the abortion wars that real action is being taken. Father

Pat's distaste for this scheme is great, but is as nothing compared to the debt he owes the Church:

> The legal and medical costs that had been incurred in securing the Petrosky's silence exceeded $200,000, which the diocese had had to bear itself, since it was no longer possible, after the debacle of the Gauté case in Louisiana, to obtain liability insurance that would pay for legal claims brought against pedophile priests. ("As well try to get flood insurance in Bangladesh," the bishop had quipped.)

The real-life Father Gauté, still serving his twenty-year sentence, is welcomed into the text, which is obviously designed to accommodate him, as it does the figures of Disch's dedication quoted above. Without such reminders of the actual scandals, evasions and legal difficulties the real church has been sunk in these several years, the reader might take Disch's tale to be an extravagance, an anti-Catholic diatribe in which the most unlikely mendacity, cynicism and vice are attributed to too many church figures to be believable.

His fervent opposition—not to say loathing—is, however clear, and operates on many levels, from skilled fun-poking and hypocrisy-deflating to a horrid delight in retribution that he makes it hard for the reader not to share. Disch, as represented by these fictions, seems not really to believe in conscience; he believes in good and evil natures, the evil being more common, though the self-promptings of good natures have a real power for those who feel them. His wicked characters feel only the dangers of exposure; they attribute their cruelties and indulgences to a supposed frailty they can do nothing about, and rarely resist their impulses; they feel shame vividly but not guilt. This seems the most non-Christian thing about these books centrally concerned with Catholicism (as all three are, *The Priest* only the most obsessively).

There are far worse things in store for Father Pat than running Birth-Right, his tough-love maternity hospital. For there is a fourth church involved in his fate (his crucifixion, not quite metaphoric); a church existing in a different space-time than the other three. To arrive at it, we must return to the book's beginning; but the book's beginning is a brilliantly and masterfully managed series of deepening revelations and downward turns that chapter by short chapter lowers us (laughing helplessly) into Disch's frightful world, and I will not analyze it; this must be one of few books where the reader's pleasure will be seriously spoiled by a description of the beginning rather than the end.

Suffice it to say that, as in the other two novels, the hopes and errors and needs of the characters meet and are entangled in a spiritual realm whose existence is largely unsuspected by them, and misunderstood when it is glimpsed. Father Pat finds himself translated—"transmentated," as he will come to find the process is called—into medieval France, where he is a Cathar-hunting cleric, Silvanus de Roquefort, Bishop of Rodez and Montpellier-le-Vieux. Changing places with the Bishop leaves him his own personality, even his own body, though afflicted with thirteenth-century pains and premature aging, and an ability to understand Languedoc French, but no other of the Bishop's memories. As in the well-known actor's dream, Father Pat has to fake it, keeping up as best he can and trying to satisfy a ferocious Dominican inquisitor just arrived from Rome, who suspects the bishop of being soft on Catharism, and who looks, to Father Pat's eye, just like Gerhardt Ober.

It's hard for Silvanus, too, though more interesting. He's found himself in Father Pat's world—more exactly, the underworld Father Pat has come to be involved in through those opening gambits—and, quite naturally, thinks he's died and gone to hell, a hell where desires are both punished and indulged. Silvanus on the loose in modern Minneapolis, getting messages from the demon TRINI-TRON and appearing as Father Pat to all, will deal roughly with more than one character, as what damnee would not?

The process of transmentation, and the precise node of this process which links Minneapolis and the now-ruined church of Montpellier-le-Vieux (if there really is such a place) is explained in the writings of A.D. Boscage, science-fiction writer and cult leader, a mix of Philip Dick, L. Ron Hubbard and famed UFO abductee Whitley Streiber (with whom Disch has had public set-tos). Boscage has himself, he claims, been a character back in Silvanus's world, and his experiences there form part of his UFO abduction theories: that a giant net of intelligences, alien or supernatural (the "Alphanes"), surround our world, and manipulate us for reasons of their own.

Father Pat—who is, as it happens, being blackmailed by Boscage's cult for reasons of *its* own, though without knowing why or how they are connected to Silvanus and the past—holds a priest's low opinion of such stuff:

> Boscage's book, *Prolegomenon to Receptivist Science*, was a virtual anthology of New Age absurdities and an obvious hoax by a rather unsophisticated hoaxer. To argue against it was as hopeless a task as bailing water out of a ruptured boat.
> The problem was that he was a passenger in the boat and the boat was in deep water.

The more interesting problem, which Father Pat will never be allowed to solve, is that Boscage's system reflects the play of supernatural power far more closely, in the universe of this book, than does Father Pat's theology. It is a common thing, in thrillers descending from the "Monk" Lewis tradition, to use the Church and its theurgies as special effects; *The Exorcist* may have been un-Catholic to its core, but within its world demonic possession followed the Church's rules, and could be defeated by the Church's means. Not here. In this book, the priests don't have a clue; the entire supernatural structure of their church is fake, their sacraments inefficacious, the whole rigamarole only a means to power and pleasure for the hierophants. Most of them know it, too, or act as though it were indisputable, whatever they say out loud.

And meanwhile all around them are more things, in heaven and on earth, than are dreamt of in their theology. Transubstantiation doesn't work, but transmentation does. At the same time there is a constant reversibility to the frights and spooks of this tale; sometimes ordinary realities turn out to mask otherworldly depths, but at other times similar supernatural events turn out to be illusory, and mask only ordinary realities. The undecidability is a constant, without any irritable striving after fact and certainty. Unlike the elaborate and smooth-running stage machinery of the supernatural in *The Businessman*, the spiritual world of *The Priest* resembles the continuous astonishing improvisation of certain classic B movies, where new material is always superseding and partially canceling out the unfolding complications of earlier premises, a process that picks up speed until the end becomes unimaginable.

The end of *The Priest* leaves the ground littered with the usual quota of corpses (including one kept for some time in a freezer, a theme, if that is the word, that also appears memorably in *The M.D.*, combined in that instance with a microwave). Death in horror novels tends to visit a broad sampling of the characters, both good and bad; the nosy get it but so do innocent bystanders, and the guilty. This evenhandedness I think impresses the young male readership of such novels as a delightful cynicism, as—in the current devalued use of the word—*ironic*. There must, though, be a core of good people who survive to the end and even profit, or the book would not be a romance. Readers of *The Businessman* will be sorry that the delightful Bing Anker, Giselle's brother and the victor of that book, is removed somewhat abruptly here, though his friend and sometime lover Father Mabbely survives, a rare decent and sympathetic cleric.

Disch brings his tale to a climax at the shrine of Blessed Konrad, which is for Father Mabbely the last straw; his occupation's gone:

> There ahead of them stood one of the Seven Wonders of the Totalitarian World... The Shrine was a perfect combination of cathedral and bunker, with a lead-gray dome of cast concrete that seemed to be sinking into the earth rather than soaring from it. Every detail was expressive of the whole, though detail, as such, had not been the architect's *forte*. It was One Big Idea, and that idea was Authority. Authority that had no use for the landscape around it, or for the people who might enter it, but only for its own swollen and ill-conceived *terribiltá*... What a bliss it would be no longer to be implicated in what that building represented! To be a priest no more and a human being again!

The body count at the Shrine is added to the numbers already accumulated, some of them dispatched, it must be admitted, rather swiftly; Blessed Konrad's guard dogs maul one sickly pregnant escapee from Birth-Right to death almost unnoticed by the reader, or the writer. For Thomas M. Disch as for Father Mabbely it may have been a relief to cease being a priest, and become again a human being—the cruel opposition he has constructed here. Indeed it is possible that this ambitious and extravagantly gifted writer is getting tired of the constraints of the horror genre. If that is so he has wrung from it more than could have been imagined, and it is to be hoped that the whole trilogy will reach, besides the usual consumers of this sort of book, those readers who will be able to grasp what an unlikely, what a large achievement it is.

"The issue always and at bottom is spiritual." Thus Dwight D. Eisenhower, in the epigraph Disch has chosen for *The Businessman*. At the end of *The Priest*, the good characters, those who have avoided being slain, gather and talk, and an attempt is made to explain the events of the plot in mundane terms of multiple personality disorder and the hypnotic effect of Boscage's fantasies. But this scene (this is of course a common trick of the genre) is followed by another, a final one, which calls into doubt all such simplifications of damnation. A similar endgame is worked to terrible effect in *The M.D.* In the world of these books, in this spiritual Minneapolis, we can only hope, not that we can avoid otherworldly threats and terrors, fates we may or may not deserve, but that around us and beyond them lies the heaven pictured in *The Businessman*, whose hardworking spirits watch over us, and where our wounds will at last be dressed: if, that is, we are both good and lucky.

1995

T.H. WHITE

*I*N ADDITION TO THE INTERIOR lists that many passionate readers make—of the Ten Greatest Books Ever Written, or of My Ten Favorite Books (not necessarily the same), or The Ten Books I would Least Want to have Missed—writers often keep another: of the Books I would Most Like to have Written. On my own short list of such books, along with *The Man who was Thursday*, *The Crying of Lot 49*, *Invisible Cities*, *Lolita*, and *A High Wind in Jamaica*, stands T. H. White's *The Once and Future King*.

White's book is in one sense an anomaly on the list, since the others share a certain stylistic virtuosity, a kind of "perfection" more easily apprehended than defined. T*he Once and Future King* is inconsistent, with passages of embarrassing slapstick, and shortcomings of a kind I am usually not patient with; and yet there it is. The reason may be that the books which make this particular list of mine do so not only because I admire them and envy the skill with which they are achieved, but because I can vividly imagine the joy and relish of their authors in creating them, the fun they had, the private pleasure. I can imagine White's most vividly of all.

He began it when he was thirty years old, and had just quit his job teaching in a public (American English: private) boy's school. He had sold his beloved Bentley and got a bicycle; he had no debts, and his little gamekeeper's cottage in the woods was fully rented; he had nothing to do. "I was wild with freedom," he wrote much later on. "I was a hawk, a falcon which had slipped its jesses. The wide air was mine again, as it ought to be in boyhood, and that year—which seems in retrospect to have passed like a flash—was one of the only seven consciously happy years I have had in all my life."

"The art of life," says Thoreau, "of a *poet*'s life, is, having nothing to do, to do something." What White did was to write *The Sword in the Stone*, the first and in most respects the most successful part of

The Once and Future King. And we can feel completely the happiness he felt in writing it.

What a reader learns who reads White's books of essays and his autobiographical writings is that the fantasy he creates in *The Once and Future King* mirrors the passions and occupations of his life. He was a passionate hunter (i.e. foxhunter, in British English) and fisherman who loved the craft and tackle and lore of those pursuits. He trained several hawks to hunt, and trained them according to the methods he found in medieval manuals of falconry—not out of mania for things medieval, but because he knew of no other way to begin; only after he had completed his goshawk's arduous training did he learn that modern falconers used simple behaviorism to achieve the same results with a tenth of the trouble—and a tenth of the passionate bonding of man to bird that the trouble entailed. (The whole heartbreaking story is told in his book *The Goshawk*.)

More directly: Merlyn's cabin was not different from the gamekeeper's cottage he lived in; he really kept an owl named Archimedes there (he'd rescued it as a baby from a brook) and baby badgers that nipped at his ankles. Half Merlyn's age, he lived backwards in his own way, escaping from the constraints of his own character into a premature absent-minded-professor character he had developed in teaching, a profession which (like Merlyn) he was devoted to.

He hayed with the local farmers, he fished for tench in the streams. The mudflats where Art lives as a wild goose are the flats where White spent hours in a shooting blind; the exquisite scenes of the geese in flight came from his own experience learning to fly a small plane in the 1930s (see his chronicle of this adventure, *England Have my Bones*). The awful poignance of the aging Arthur dreaming that wars would end when men could one day fly like the geese, and could know how negligible are the borders they have drawn on the earth and defend so passionately, must come from a similar hopeless hope the young White felt.

White loved the insides of books, and he also loved the natural world. Of course much fantasy literature is filled with Nature of a sort, with forests and animals and weather, and readers of fantasy are eager for it. It is common for a reader of fantasy to export the matter of his reading into the world he lives in—export the emblematic beasts and forests and the symbol-freighted techniques (falconry, archery, woodcraft)—and by means of them enlarge the meaning or at least the affect of his diurnal round. White really did the opposite: he imported into his fictions the real crafts he had learned, the real beasts he knew, the real relations between animals and men which he himself had.

Thus the animals into which the boy Arthur is transformed, though they can speak, are not fantasy animals or mythic animals at all, not the wolves or Ents of Tolkien but the ordinary animals of de-divinized post-Darwinian ethology, *our* animals; and this renews their symbolic power within the Arthurian story. As Lytton Strachey noted about the speaking animals of La Fontaine's fables, they "are not simply animals with the minds of human beings; they are something more complicated and amusing; they are animals with the minds which human beings would certainly have, if one could suppose them transformed into animals."

Something similar happens in White's treatment of the English Middle Ages: he imports into his Arthurian fantasy the historical Middle Ages he had studied and loved, and by a simple trick enriches the fantasy realm he is creating with the actualities he obviously relishes teaching us about. The trick is effective partly because of its obviousness, like a shock effect in a movie achieved by nothing more than film run backward: White simply pretends that Arthur's rule extends over the whole course of the medieval period, from shortly after the Conquest to the Wars of the Roses, and that it is the other kings—the Richards and Henrys and Edwards—that are the mythical ones.

This allows White to talk directly to the reader as a teacher, pondering with him the right translation of medieval terms of art, finding familiar analogues, quoting real handbooks of falconry and hunting, and getting away with anachronistic jokes: "The battle of Crecy was won on the playing fields of Camelot," and so on. He can be nostalgic about medieval social relations, ironically nostalgic about the weather ("It was July, and real July weather, such as they had in Old England") and get away with it, because it is Arthur's England he's nostalgic about. What is mysterious is that though it used chiefly to amuse, this trick ends by deepening the poignance of the tale; the decline of Arthur's realm, and White's sadness at it, borrows affect from the real historical passing of an order that White mourned.

Like many English lives—like White's perhaps—his book seems richest in its beginnings, and not only darkens but grows thin as it progresses. Children and childhood call up his best efforts, not only the essentially happy childhood of the Wart but the terrible childhoods of the sons of Morgan LeFay. Lancelot's baffled desire to be good had such deep roots in White's nature that he made it effective, but when he approached the intensity of grown-up sexual passion that joined Lancelot and Guinevere he faltered.

White's own orientation was homosexual, and he suffered from that aberration that transforms sexual desire into the impulse to cause pain—a genuine aberration, I believe, and quite different from the largely histrionic excitements of S&M. In any case the impulses he felt frightened White away from any kind of sexual encounter for much of his life, and pushed him into self-exile in rural Ireland (no country can dampen sexual ardors of any kind more thoroughly) or Scotland. The greatest love of his life was an Irish setter, whose death he mourned extravagantly and, though he kept other dogs, never got over. It is characteristic that the muddle and pain caused by sexuality are clear in the affair of Lancelot and Guinevere but never the exaltation; nothing that happens between them equals the heart-tearing moment in *The Sword in the Stone* when the King's huntsman Master Twyti puts down his dog Beaumont, whose spine has been broken by a boar.

There are other lapses in the later parts of the book. White can no more rise to the religious mysticism of the Grail legend than to Courtly Love; both are beyond his ken, and seem to be beyond the ken of his knights as well. (It's too bad that the Arthur stories he uses are exclusively the Christianized ones; there are Grails and Grail legends in other sources that don't turn on Christian myth and monkish ideals of "purity", and White might have responded better to them. Wolfram von Eschenbach's Parzival is a married man.) The comedy, especially in the later parts, grows tiresome, and more tiresome I would think for an English reader: the John-Bull old knights with Edwardian doncha-know accents and mild-eyed twits like King Pellinore are at least interestingly outlandish to Americans, and not simply the stuff of old *Punch* cartoons.

Never mind: by the end the tale itself seems to take control, enormous engine of destiny; White must have his characters meet the fates they must meet, sometimes cruel and terrible ones that no author would think of assigning to such comic characters as Pellinore. A thoroughgoing late-medieval cruelty settles over the story, and the Wat's boyhood in the Forest Sauvage becomes the infinitely precious world that will be lost entirely when Arthur is taken to Avalon, not to be restored until, in some manner that this plain-style Arthur cannot grasp, he returns. I have read the brief scene in Arthur's tent at the book's end a dozen times, when the boy Tom Malory promises to tell the truth about the old King's reign, and never without tears.

The Once and Future King was by far White's most successful book, and made him rich and relatively happy. (He liked being lionized in his later years and even loved the musical *Camelot*, to my ears and eyes exactly the phony theatrical romanticizing that *The Once and Future King* is not.) But it is far from being his only book. There is a genuine science fiction novel too, out of print as far as I know, called *The Master*: a philosophical romance about eternal life, world peace and other things, with charms of its own and some resemblance to Jules Verne. There are the writings about fishing, hunting, Ireland, Scotland, hawks, history and other things collected in *The Godstone and the Blackymore*. And there is *Mistress Masham's Repose*, one of those small classics that ends up in the Childrens department and there lives long, known to a select society of smart children, unknown to all others: as happened for a while to Madeleine L'Engle's *A Wrinkle In Time*—and Tolkien too, for that matter.

The central notion of *Mistress Masham's Repose* is that Gulliver on his return to England brought back (as he intended) several Lilliputian natives, along with some sheep, cows and horses; and that they escaped from their intended bondage in a traveling circus, hid themselves, and have been keeping themselves hidden up to the present time (1946, when the book was written). The idea, once grasped, is so natural that the reader seems almost to have thought it up himself; and White enriches it wonderfully by having the place where the Lilliputians took refuge be a vast 18th-century estate, "built by a friend of the poet Pope's, and . . . surrounded by Vistas,

Obelisks, Pyramids, Columns, Temples, Rotundas, and Palladian Bridges." It is within the hollow columns of a classical gazebo built on a little island of the estate, called Mistress Masham's Repose, that the Lilliputians have been living.

Within a far smaller compass, *Mistress Masham's Repose* allows White to indulge a fondness for the eighteenth century as *The Once and Future King* did his love of the Middle Ages, in the same chatty smart-teacher mode: "Maria laid her bark alongside the end of a larch, and tied it up so that it could not drift away—an Inconvenience, as Gulliver tells us, which all prudent Mariners take special Care to provide against." (The Lilliputians, when they appear, all speak Swift's English, of course, with capitalized Nouns.)

But the story of young Maria's discovery of the little people didn't excite White only because it was fun, though it is; he wanted to think about moral difficulties, ones similar to those he thinks so hard about in *The Once and Future King*: tyranny and freedom, resisting wickedness, using others for one's own ends. Like Arthur's, Maria's problems (she is innately tempted to rule, kindlily of course, over the little people she has discovered) are mediated by a wise, absent-minded, scholarly and aged teacher, not so unworldly as he seems, who lives in a cluttered cabin in the woods. It continues to intrigue me how often good writers have only a single book to write, and write it over and over.

It is the force of White's moral convictions that make this such a wonderful book to come across when you're young, and they remain compelling when one's own moral life has grown shadowed and complex with grown-up evasions and compromises.

About the villains in the story, White says first: "Maria's governess was a Miss Brown. She had been appointed by the local vicar, who was Maria's guardian. Both the vicar and the governess were so repulsive that it is difficult to write about them fairly... It is difficult but important to believe that this precious pair may have been trying to do the best they could, considering the kind of people they were." He gives them not one jot more than his own sense of right compels him to—but he gives them that. When this loathsome couple (the worse sadists for being certain of their own moral rightness) threaten Maria with harm unless she lets them in on the secret of the little people she has found (they want to sell them, of course) White tells us the only way to resist such people when you are in their power is "to tell them the truth, and to face them, and to let them see how much you hate them plainly, so long as you can make them understand that you will hurt them if you can. It frightens them away."

T.H. White seems himself to have been a passionately good man; the goodness may have been hardwon, the result of his struggle to overcome what he saw as the temptation to give pain (like the heroic goodness of his Ill-made Knight, Lancelot) and the struggle may be what gives such simple moral force to his writing. In his last years he lived on the tiny Channel island of Alderney (more exile) and there he took care of an assortment of mentally and physically handicapped people who had wandered into his life, who bored and confused White's literary visitors but with whom White was unfailingly patient. He died in this month, twenty-six years ago. Sylvia Townsend Warner (*Kingdoms of Elfin*) has written an engaging and touching biography.

1990

VLADIMIR NABOKOV

THE MAGICIAN'S DOUBTS by Michael Wood, and THE STORIES OF VLADIMIR NABOKOV, edited by Dimitri Nabokov

*M*ICHAEL WOOD BEGINS HIS study of Vladimir Nabokov with a precis of his author's career that resembles (consciously no doubt) the chilling one-paragraph summation of the hero's life that opens Nabokov's novel *Laughter in the Dark*. "There was once a Russian writer, let's call him V., who was prodigiously gifted: learned, intelligent, observant, inventive," Wood begins, and he ends: "A scandalous book brought him late and surprising fame and wealth, and he moved to a hotel in Switzerland, where he continued to write, enjoying both glory and privacy, and died at the age of 78, a man who told his son that he had accomplished what he wished in art and life."

As *Laughter in the Dark* has it, there is room on any gravestone to contain—"bound in moss"—a man's life (and Wood reminds us that Nabokov's stone in Montreux says only *Vladimir Nabokov écrivain 1899-1977*) but "detail is always welcome." Wood's eye and ear for revealing detail are acute, and in the course of his book the satisfactory, even gratifying, tale told in the opening paragraphs will undergo a complex and fascinating—a very Nabokovian—shifting and doubling as Wood contends with the great shade. He wants, he says, "to suggest that this life itself is really sort of a fable, as all achieved careers are: exemplary, purified, haunting."

The central fact of Nabokov's career, is, of course, loss: the loss of his homeland and his language, the one an involuntary loss, the other, Wood says, not quite so involuntary: "Nabokov didn't *lose* his language, he foreswore the use of it for the purpose which most mattered to him," and the choice became a destiny. Nabokov had to (or believed he had to) give up his first language in order to create himself as a writer in his second. He "found, through his very loss, a fabulous, freaky, singing, acrobatic, unheard-of English," and found that "the second language could flower for him only at the cost of the first." It may be, as Wood says, that though you may have more than one language, you can love but one at a time.

Nabokov claimed over and over that his terrible losses did not matter, because nothing is lost to the heroic consciousness, which the tyrants and time cannot touch. Wood will show that loss cannot be rejected without being named and acknowledged, that the haughty and inhumanly gay writer Nabokov projected was "too self-sufficient, too armored against doubt to have written Nabokov's later novels." Wood finds instead a writer of considerable, if inconsistent, moral courage, one who discovered in his own losses "the intimate meanings of uncertainty, of exclusion, disarray, clumsiness and poverty," a writer who "finds the humanity the first writer was so keen to hide."

"Texts we care about will both resist and reward us; not necessarily in that order." Nabokov, famous teaser, illusionist, layer and brusher-away of tracks, seems often enough to be laughing at us as we stumble after him; if we can't keep up, he seems to say, we should not have set out. But Wood finds that "doubt is what we find lurking in his apparent assurance, like death in Arcady."

The reader will have collected all the insights quoted above, and others, before ever leaving Wood's brief Preface. How Wood makes good on them through the length of his book cannot be explicated in the space here allotted, though the temptation to try is strong. Wood brings to Nabokov a kind of compassion I think Nabokov would have found unsettling, and it permits him to give to us a Nabokov we had not seen before; those of us who have always found Nabokov and his fiction a somewhat guilty pleasure, who have wondered how we can be so moved by Nabokov's solipsistic pedants and self-deceivers, will find here many reasons both for the guilt and for the pleasure. The only difficulty, only it is not really a difficulty but an invitation to delight, is that Wood pushes us relentlessly back toward the books, makes us dissatisfied with what we remember of them even if we think we remember a great deal.

Wood's study appears in the United States at the same moment as Nabokov's collected stories, edited by his son and frequent collaborator in translation, Dimitri Nabokov. Thirteen have never been published in book form before, and represent what Nabokov himself called "the bottom of the barrel," an idiom his son interprets as meaning all the remainder of any worth; a few of the new stories, however, do hint at the colloquial connotation of the phrase. The very first, *The Wood-sprite*, is quite poor, and others are best described as slender.

Many of stories in this volume, early and late, deal with the themes of loss, language, and the self-deceiving, self-creating narrator-author that Wood explicates (*The Leonardo, The Admiralty Spire, Cloud, Castle, Lake*) though of course in one or two dimensions rather than the four or five Nabokov can achieve in the novels. Most of those written in Russian exist for readers of English only in Nabokov's later transformations, adding a further level of illusionism. One (*Mademoiselle O*) appears here as a story, and in a slightly different form as part of Nabokov's autobiographical work *Speak, Memory*. Two (*Ultima Thule* and *Solus Rex*) are chapters or parts of a never-completed novel in Russian, whose themes and tricks appear in several of Nabokov's fictions in English: I wish Wood had included them in his study.

One of the stories written in English, and one which Wood studies at some length, is *The Vane Sisters*, whose last paragraph includes an acrostic message from the two dead sisters to the narrator, who fails to perceive it, though the reader is expected to. Nabokov had to explain the joke to Katherine White, the very alert story editor of the *New Yorker*, and as Wood says, "If explanations are needed, someone has failed, either writer or reader, or perhaps both." Nabokov demanded an inordinate amount from readers, even as he did his duty in amusing and engaging them (a duty many demanding writers see as beneath them). Wood quotes the "august and strenuous ideal of readership" Nabokov put forward in the introduction to his translation of *Eugene Onegin*: "Unless these and other mechanisms and every other detail of the text are consciously assimilated, *Eugene Onegin* cannot be said to exist in the reader's mind."

"These despotic phrases call for a long commentary," Wood says, and his book is one such; another, of course, is Nabokov's own fiction, short and long, which demands, or gives the illusion of demanding, just such a reader. Anyone who writes now in expectation of having such demands on a reader's attention (and time!) met must appear hopelessly quixotic; Nabokov in his arrogance stands like a last great headland above a beach all but washed away.

The advance copy of *The Stories of Vladimir Nabokov* is flecked with misprints, of a peculiar modern kind: the kind where the clever but wholly witless computer lets stand a spelling error that resulted in a true but wrong word—"it" for "is," "midgets" for "midges." A kind of misprint Nabokov would surely have enjoyed playing tricks with. They are very hard to detect.

1996

VN: THE LIFE AND ART OF VLADIMIR NABOKOV by Andrew Field, and THE ENCHANTER by Vladimir Nabokov, translated by Dimitri Nabokov

It's widely noticed how often life imitates art; it is certainly true that the literary life imitates literature with an often vengeful exactness. Vladimir Nabokov's fiction was full of mistaken, mad or dreaming biographers, mismatched with subjects who inhabited different universes altogether. Now Nabokov himself is caught in the net of a strangely antipathetic biographer, who in turn catches himself up in some very Nabokovian tangles.

Vladimir Nabokov's journey through three geographical and spiritual realms has an epic quality even if it is not taken strictly in the terms Nabokov set. There was, first, his childhood in pre-revolutionary Russia—the beloved child of wealthy, kind and apparently happy parents, avid reader, football and tennis player, puppy-lover, butterfly collector. Next, exile in Crimea, Berlin, Paris; the creation of himself as a writer in Russian but not in Russia; the recreation of his lost childhood as a realm of art. Andrew Field, in writing of the apparent joy with which Nabokov set about this task, uses the word "optimism", but it was not optimism; it was the brave joy of tragic understanding. As the small émigré community who alone could read his books grew inexorably smaller, he might cease to be read altogether, and yet he wrote.

Then America, and the recreation of himself as an American writer, which required the transformation of his lost Russia into allegories of the experience of loss itself: the unanswerable desires, the wild hopes, the self-delusions, the cold comforts of dream and art.

Andrew Field has done years of research into these various journeys, has talked to nearly everyone who would talk to him and gathered every story that could be gathered. He has small. gifts for narrative, however, and his writing is efficient at best, irremediably klutzy at frequent worst: "The Nabokovs all married not just for money but, without any doubt, with money in mind as well." "Narcissus [Nabokov] could in a very real sense create reflected worlds at least as diabolically intricate as God's." Field uses "workmanlike" when surely he means "workaday;" he wants "fatidic" to mean "fateful" when all it really means is "prophetic." He expresses "lack of interest" by the word *"dis*interest" (his own unfortunate italics). It's odd that someone who must have been drawn to Nabokov at least in part through love of language should find it such an intractable medium himself.

Then there is Field's vision of Nabokov's life in art, which has certainly grown and altered since his early Nabokov studies. He announces often—almost gleefully—that Nabokov ardently protested this or that suggestion which Field made to him, about connections between his life and his art, or possible literary influences on him, some of which Field seems to have lighted on with wilful perversity—like Dostoevsky ("not a little unacknowledged borrowing") or D.H. Lawrence ("it really cannot be avoided").

Field's literary analyses culminate in a reading of *Lolita* so mistaken as to be nearly unintelligible. Using Freudian categories (which Nabokov of course despised) Field claims to have discovered that "an important subject" of the novel is "Humbert's struggle against homosexuality." It would seem that only someone unable to be touched at all by the central passion of Nabokov's greatest book could possibly entertain such a dazzlingly dumb idea. Field supports it by reducing some sublime jokes to cinders on the grim grill of Freudian disunderstanding.

The most dramatic discovery of Field's Freudian sleuthing, though—and gratifying indeed it must have been to him—comes when; by careful examination of the excised salutations of some letters of Nabokov to his mother which Field was permitted to see, Field determines that Nabokov privately addressed his own mother as—Lolita! The missing name is "about seven letters long," and Field can see the telltale top of the "t" above the space.

Nonsense, says Nabokov's son Dimitri. The excised name is not Lolita at all in the originals (which Dimitri has) but *radost* ("dearest"). The Cyrillic "t" *has* no top or tail, anyway—and "Lolita" is only six letters long.

Dimitri Nabokov's rebuttal of this and other absurdities he sees in Field's book ("an odd concoction of rancor, adulation, innuendo and outright factual error") comes in the postscript to his new translation of *The Enchanter*, his father's last extensive piece of Russian prose, now appearing for the first time.

The Enchanter is the story which Nabokov describes in the afterword to *Lolita* as the original of that book, and which he thought then had been lost or destroyed. It was written in Paris, where the story takes place; in it, a middle-aged pedophile (unnamed) spies on girls in a park, and contrives to marry the sickly mother of the most enchanting of them, in order to be near the girl. After the mother dies, he attempts to enjoy the girl secretly as she sleeps in a country hotel he has taken her to. The attempt is a disaster, and the distraught pervert, fleeing the hotel, is killed by a (heavily prefigured) midnight truck.

Borges once wrote an essay about how the very existence of Kafka brought into being the "Kafka-esque" qualities of writers who long preceded him. *The Enchanter* closely resembles the first part of *Lolita*, not only in gross outline but in the minute planning of suspense, comic reversal, ironic fulfillment, hope and despair; but in this excellent and very "Nabokovian" translation, it has the effect not of a foreshadowing but of an imitation, a flattish, deflated, occasionally brilliant pastiche, stealing its pale fire from the sun of the later book.

It is written, unlike *Lolita*, in the third person—a crucial difference, I contend—and its unnamed girl never comes alive in the cooler regard of third-person narration. It lacks, too, one enormous dimension that the novel has: America. The story's single trip through an unremarked French countryside becomes, in *Lolita*, those heartbreaking, epic crossings of Nabokov's "lovely, trustful, dreaming, enormous country," transformed by Humbert into "umber and black Humberland."

For Humbert is—and the sadsack hero of the old story, despite its title, is finally not—an enchanter. His magic is in his language, in his projection of a world of words for his own uses. Like all black magic, Humbert's depends on winning the participation of the enchanted: not Lolita, who is not ever truly enchanted, but the reader. Humbert's magic consists in causing us, by the power of words alone, to participate in his desire for Lolita—a desire so compelling that it will explain everything, excuse everything.

Both Dimitri Nabokov and Andrew Field go to some lengths to make certain we understand that Nabokov did not condone perversion, that his works condemn their obsessed protagonists, that Nabokov was not indifferent to the sufferings of their victims. But this is beside the point. Nabokov's crime—if it is one—lies not in condoning or indulging a perversion, but in indulging his own power to make us share it: and for no more moral reason, either, than to show that he could do it. For that there can be no excuse; nor, I think, would Nabokov want one made.

In any case he is now, like all the great dead, consigned to a peculiar purgatory, and in the hands of his biographers. I will not soon forget one horripilating moment recounted by Field. Nabokov and Vera, his wife, were being interviewed by Field, and Vera was resisting Field's attempts to probe her private life. Why could she just not be left out of the book altogether? "With laughter and tears" (I suspect that Field means "with tears of laughter," but let it stand, let it stand) Nabokov cried out, "You can't help being represented! We're too far gone! It's too late!"

1986

THE MAN FROM THE U.S.S.R. AND OTHER PLAYS

For every reader there are certain writers whose passing occasions a special sadness: now there will be no more of *those,* those exquisite gift-boxes full of unguessable surprises. Anyone who felt that way about Vladimir Nabokov cannot help being cheered by the introduction Dmitri Nabokov has contributed to this new collection of his father's plays and essays on the theater: for these sound like the real Nabokovian thing.

It's not quite so. Dmitri Nabokov stresses the kinship of these four plays—one full-length farce, a shorter and less describable piece, and two one-acters—with Nabokov's novels and stories, and traces themes and motifs which they have in common: doubling and mirroring of characters, expeditions, return to Russia or the dream-memory of a Russia that might be returned to, the artifice of actuality and the actuality of illusion. But perhaps only a son's—or a critic's—eye could discern even a pale Nabokovian fire in these pieces.

The farce—*The Event*—is the best of them. An egotistical portrait painter and his unfaithful wife learn that an old lover of the wife's, whom the painter succeeded, has been let out early from prison. His crime was the attempted murder of painter and wife, and he once vowed to finish the job. Panic, recrimination, suspense, while a crowd of foolish persons keep arriving for tea, unable to take seriously the painter's certainty of his mortal danger. And yes, there *are* doublings and dream-logic, and there are grotesques of the kind that Nabokov inherited from Gogol, and there is some amusing interplay of the theatrical illusion with a sense of life itself as a kind of theatrical illusion. But the language the characters are made to speak, in Dmitri Nabokov's translation, is quite unspeakable even by figments, a weird melange of an unnatural mid-Atlantic or translator's English with American slang of many periods, not all of it used exactly correctly. "Drive me bananas," "bumped off," "and how!," "hick-town" (meaning "small-time") sound strange indeed in the mouths of characters also liable to say lines like "If I don't get the money, I'll know they want my ruin."

The other plays also suffer from this kind of translatorese, and suffer worse, for they are slighter things. The title play, in which a man from the U.S.S.R. is reflected differently in the hopes and fears of a group of Russian emigres in the Berlin of the '20s, seems to be missing the essential ingredient which it needs to function at all, and that is an audience of Russian emigres of the '20s, who would supply all that the little play goes without: context, resonance, emotional force. The two one-acters, in a very blank kind of verse, are inconsequential: unless the original Russian contains much vanished magic, our author's light was still under its bushel when these juvenilia were composed.

Included with the plays are two essays. In *Playwriting* Nabokov claims that theatrical effect depends completely on the actors onstage never acknowledging that they are being watched, never becoming aware of the audience. It is the essence of theater that the audience is aware of the actors, but has no power over them and their world, and that the actors are unaware that they are on a stage watched by other people, though they have the power of moving, amusing, transforming those other people.

Pronouncements like that ignore great stretches of theatrical history, including Shakespeare, but are necessary to the Nabokovian metaphysic and manner, as in *The Event*, when the painter describes a vision he has had for a painting: "Try to imagine that this wall is missing," he says to his wife, meaning the Fourth Wall, which is of course missing, "and instead there is a black abyss and what looks like an audience in a dim theater..." But no, he decides, maybe it's a bad idea: "Let there be a wall again."

The other essay *(The Tragedy of Tragedy)* is built upon an amusing but quite unfair equivocation, confusing the iron laws of Fate in classical tragedy with the wooden ones of old-fashioned stage convention. It's a plea for a kind of drama based not on fate at all but on the paradoxical laws—discernible in puns, in mirrors, in coincidences—of bright and pitiless chance. This is, again, less relevant to the history of theater than to the Nabokovian enterprise itself, fiction, drama, poetry or prose. In fact the thought occurs that what we have here, in the filial piety of the introductions, the tin-eared translations, the inadequate though occasionally intriguing plays, and the quirky essays, is the base matter for a wonderful Nabokov novel: a novel his ghost is somewhere writing, and that we will never read.

1997

ANTHONY BURGESS

THE KINGDOM OF THE WICKED

Simone Weil once noted an insoluble literary problem: that in literature goodness tends to appear banal, dull and colorless, and evil seems thrilling, fulfilling and rich—while in life it's just the reverse. This problem must necessarily be hardest to solve when the novel sets an enterprise of absolute, even divine, goodness against one of history's great examples of wickedness, as Anthony Burgess's new novel does.

The Kingdom of the Wicked takes up where Mr. Burgess's *Man of Nazareth* left off, with the apostles of Jesus in a state of dismay and wild hope after the Crucifixion. It's narrated by the son of the skeptical Jew who narrated the earlier novel, and follows very closely the events related in the *Acts of the Apostles* in the Bible: how the tiny Nazarene sect was persecuted by orthodox Judaism and the Roman Empire, how it became a religion chiefly of Gentiles, and how Peter and the original leadership were eclipsed by the vigorous evangelizing of Paul.

That's the Good. The Evil is taken out of those horrific (and tendentious) Roman histories of Tacitus and Suetonius that tell of the lurid misdeeds and endless bloodlust of the last Claudian emperors and their wives, Caligula, Nero, Messalina and the rest. Mr. Burgess—or his narrator, rather—retells these scandals with straightforward credulity, just as he retells the miracles and blessings that accompanied the disciples' missions. He takes exception to very little, and since the style of the book is no careful counterfeit of classical writings, as Marguerite Yourcenar's *Memoirs of Hadrian* was, but is written in a very modern and Burgess-like voice, it seems that it is Mr. Burgess who takes no exception to the extraordinary story he has to tell.

But if the moral oppositions and the pious anecdotes are not different from those of a dozen old novels—*The Robe, The Silver Chalice, Quo Vadis?*—the tone is utterly lacking in the solemnity that once seemed mandatory. The supper at Emmaus, the Pentecost, the healings and visitations and exorcisms are completely matter-of-fact, and some—the raising of Dorcas from the dead is one—approach slapstick. As one solution to the Weil problem, this method holds the attention, but the fire of mystic apprehension, the sense of living in the last days before the world's destruction and renewal, is missing almost entirely from these Christians. And this earthbound quality paradoxically makes the story seem even more extraordinary: sometimes, indeed, downright unlikely.

Any novel that includes not only the razing of the Temple but the conquest of Britain and the burning of Rome *and* the destruction of Pompeii has included too much. *(The Kingdom of the Wicked* was written in preparation for a TV miniseries.) It can only be carried forward by a kind of shorthand: two-dimensional characters, "kaleidoscopic" action, clichés of confrontation and conflict. Mr. Burgess constructs one of those historical-novel subplots about representative people who turn up everywhere and get in on everything, and when Paul bumps into the Emperor Nero who is out on a toot in disguise, coincidence is stretched to television lengths.

The Kingdom of the Wicked is not Burgess at the top of his bent. Unlike one or two of his other historical pieces *(Nothing Like the Sun, Napoleon Symphony)* it can't be immediately classed as literature. You might call it glitterature. But Mr Burgess does expend much wealth of language, wit and energy, and marshals masses of intriguing and funny historical detail, and in the end his cartoons, like the two-dimensional cartoons in a Dickens novel, pile up to make an almost three-dimensional world.

1985

THE PIANOPLAYERS

This is Anthony Burgess' best novel in years, better in some ways than his justly acclaimed *Earthly Powers*. That novel was a big, powerful bestseller that was also a subtle parody of a big, powerful bestseller. *The Pianoplayers* is thoroughly genuine, a return to the milieu of Burgess' youth and in certain ways to the mode of his earlier novels. It has seemed in the last few years that Burgess had got tired of fashioning novels, had ceased to give the job his full attention. But on the evidence of this book, he has lost none of his old powers, and gained a few new ones besides.

The pianoplayers (yes, one word) of the title are Ellen Henshaw, who is telling this story with artful artlessness into a tape recorder, and her father Billy, who is the last silent-movie accompanist in his part of northern England, forced out of work by the coming of sound. It's Billy who insists he's a pianoplayer, not a pianist; his is a craft, one he's proud of and wants to pass on to his motherless daughter (Mum died in the flu epidemic of 1918).

"He was never stuck," says Ellen of her father's skill as movie accompanist; Billy plays not only for the feature but for the advertisements ("Roast Beef of Old England" is good for a butcher) and the newsreel ("Oh How I Love to Be Beside the Seaside" for a story on "Record Crowds at Margate"). Comedy he likes least—"very fast ragtime style, no real letting up at all, not even for the odd kiss and cuddle."

Ellen and Billy inhabit—truly inhabit, in this most circumstantial and vivid of Burgess's recent books—a seedy semi-demimonde, 1920s and '30s working-class industrial England of rooming houses and fish-and-chip shops, grim Catholic schools and the drab cinemas and seaside "resorts" where Billy works. I can't think of a more dispiriting literary milieu, and Billy Henshaw, unwell, incipiently alcoholic, never to fulfill his great talents or even retain his trade, ought to be a tragic, or at least sad, character; but the book is instead enormously cheerful, and the Henshaws are a good-natured and loving twosome, whom the author never idealizes and never, ever condescends to.

Out of a job for good, Billy seeks for a way to take care of his teenaged daughter. He makes one final Depression-era stab at big money, volunteering for an endurance piano-playing marathon, a month without stopping, playing day and night, only two hours in 24 to sleep. The marathon is an astonishing tour-de-force for Billy—and for his author—as Billy plays on for pages and pages: "Music of Monsters (dad's fists going like mad in a like feeble way all over the keys), I Love Little Pussy Her Coat Is So Warm, Memories of Last Christmas (popular carols), In a Chinese Temple Garden, Pomp and Circumference March (the one with Land of Hope and Glory) . . . and a hell of a lot more, and all from memory, not one note of music in front of him."

A hell of a lot more, but Billy doesn't make it through 30 days. His death at the keyboard leaves Ellen alone—but not helpless. She's already on her way to making a living with a different instrument—her own body.

Recruited for a high-class Catholic academy in Belgium, Ellen in all innocence (but without much surprise, either) finds herself being trained, like Colette's Gigi, to be a highly paid "companion" to wealthy French gentlemen. It's Ellen's conviction that the only men who ought to be allowed access to that powerful instrument, a woman's sexuality, are those who know how to play it. She sets herself to be their teacher, and turns instruction into a long and lucrative career, complete with franchised sex schools and TV fame. Her son is a pianoplayer too, his desires frustrated by his dragonish wife and mum-in-law; but her grandson, reincarnating Billy, will become a real pianist at last.

This second part of the novel is perhaps more slapdash than the first, but part of the pleasure of reading a Burgess novel is seeing what varying materials he will try to stitch into a whole. In "The Pianoplayers" we get—in addition to the masses of old music—instruction in playing the piano; menus of a 1930s workingman's cafe; a violin method (predating Suzuki) complete with sample practice piece; a well known "urban folktale" (The Dead Grandmother) told at hilarious length but with a conclusion different from (and inferior to) the usual American one; and much more.

Whatever other ambitions they have had, Burgess's best novels have always been compelling entertainments. His comic novels are completely lacking in that *Schadenfreude* that shadows the Cruel School of British comedy, the Waughs and Mitfords and Amises. His polymathy and love of odd lore, his verbal ingenuities, are continually engaging, but so are the affection and fellow-feeling he so generously creates for his sometimes limited, often unwise, frequently unhealthy men and women, like the pianoplayers of this novel. If the phrases hadn't been long ago rendered worthless by the writers and reviewers of meretricious junk, I would say that *The*

Pianoplayers is a terrific read, a page-turner. I really could not put it down till I was done.

1986

ANY OLD IRON

The reviewer pales before the job of even mentioning all that Anthony Burgess has put into *Any Old Iron*. The central family of the book is that of David Jones, a Welsh runaway, sailor and cook, who survives the sinking of the Titanic, a piece of luck so extreme that he thinks it may have drained all such good luck from the rest of his life. He and his strong, beautiful Russian wife, whom he inherited from the owner of a Russian restaurant in Brooklyn where he washed ashore, produce three Russian-Welsh-English-speaking children: Reginald Morrow Jones (named for a Welsh nationalist writer his father admired), a boy fierce, visionary, a little mad; his brother Dan, not bright but greatly strong; and their sister, the beautiful and even stronger Beatrix.

These three are bound up with a brother and sister, Jews of Manchester, the stolid dark-minded Harry (who narrates this novel, though in Burgess's unmistakable voice) and Zipporah, percussionist, beautiful and strong. (The women of this book are alike single-minded, clear-eyed and commanding, almost beyond the ken of their less purposeful men.) Reg Jones marries Zipporah; Harry is once commanded to bed by Beatrix, and loves her without return ever after.

Together and apart, in Wales, in Manchester, Gibraltar, Petersburg (and Leningrad)—nearly round the world—these families act and suffer through not only the Titanic disaster, but the First World War, the Russian Revolution, the Spanish Civil War (Reg volunteers), the Second World War (Dan walks from a prison camp in East Germany to Odessa), and the foundation of Israel (Harry becomes an expert in terrorism and bodyguard to Chaim Weizmann.)

This sort of immense buffet of historical anecdote, great men encountered briefly, turning points of the century witnessed and horrors endured, is of course offered in dozens of thick books published every year and never read again. The difference is that Burgess is not a leaden slogger through Our Times, but a man born under Mercury, natal star of writers and liars; his love of words and what can be found inside them and built out of them is deep and infectious, and his characters share it to an unlikely degree. The characteristic Burgess novel is a series of set-pieces, constructed like floats out of linguistic arcana, historical facts and fancies, evocative place-names, all connected by a swift and supple prose that stops for little and yet is so fully-packed that nothing seems left out. (Almost nothing: inevitably the Burgess cast can seem somewhat chivvied along by the Burgess verbal energy, and undergo transformations or reversals too sudden to be digested, by them or the reader.)

In a review of a new edition of the *Oxford Companion to English Literature*, Burgess showed how an entire novel might be constructed out of the entries on two facing pages of that wonderful miscellany. (He didn't say that he himself would be the only novelist who would be tempted to do it, or who might bring it off.) The brightest and strangest thread in this big loose fabric is just such a yoking of unlikelihoods: a story of resurgent Welsh nationalism, at once poignant and preposterous, and the discovery of what might be the sword of King Arthur and the stone from which it was drawn. The sword once belonged to Attila the Hun; the Benedictines took it for safekeeping to Monte Cassino; the Nazis shipped it to Germany with other plunder, and the Russians stole it from them and put it in the Hermitage. A string of outlandish and wholly absorbing adventures returns the sword to Wales from exile in Russia, to the Jones family pub in Gwent.

The Welsh nationalists, a band of incompetents too decently ordinary even to be very harmful (at least by the time the book ends; the same could once have been said of the Irish insurgents) are only the vivid fictional instance of a general truth Burgess wants to affirm: that the past cannot be avenged. The crime is in the past, and the punishment is in the present, qualitatively different; it cannot be justice to inflict it, however compelling to the heart vengeance can be.

Reg Jones, a man thirsty for vengeance of several kinds, in the end returns the supposed sword of Arthur to the unknowable darkness where it belongs: he throws it (of course) into a lake. His brother Dan, who goes with him, disposes of the family burden of luck good and bad in the same water. It is one of the most moving scenes Burgess has written, dark as a dream yet luminous with that wisdom about common things that age is supposed to bring and rarely does.

There is not a page of *Any Old Iron* that is mistakable for the work of any other writer, and not a page without some pleasure in it. There is the added gratification of watching an old master (who only a few years ago seemed ready to break his staff) performing with undiminished vigor. And this may also be the one book of his many books that can, at one or two moments, bring tears to a reader's eyes. At least it did to mine.

1988

ENDERBY'S DARK LADY

There is a Ph.D. thesis to be written—well, maybe a term paper—on the tendency of our contemporary novelists to create characters who write parodic, trashy or otherwise inverted versions of their creators' earlier works. John Irving and Vladimir Nabokov are only the first to come to mind. Now comes Anthony Burgess's latest novel, in which Burgess's character Enderby sets about writing slapdash versions of *Nothing Like the Sun,* one of Burgess's finest novels.

In *Enderby's Dark Lady,* Mr. Enderby, the expatriate (Tangier, Morocco) English poet of late middle age and waning powers, has published in a literary magazine a story about Shakespeare. It tells of how Shakespeare and Ben Jonson got involved in the Gunpowder Plot and the King James translation of the Bible and how Shakespeare sneaks a mention of himself into the 46th Psalm. On the strength of this jape, Enderby is chosen to write the book for an American musical about the Bard, somehow celebratory of our Bicentennial, to premiere at the Peter Brook Theater in Terrebasse, Indiana (Burgess does not go far for his names).

The musical has been funded by a rich eccentric woman named Schoenbaum. That is also, probably not coincidentally, the name of an eminent Shakespeare scholar who has said dismissive things about Burgess's Shakespeare theories. The musical is to be scored, produced and acted by an array of subliterate, egotistical, foul-mouthed and trendy Americans of a sort not unfamiliar to us in novels by highly literate Englishmen. But then enters April Elgar, a black American pop singing star and Enderby's own dark lady. Through the vagaries of theatrical disaster and Anglo-American incomprehension (not really as much fun as it might have been), there shines darkly an intriguing meditation, or musing, on the Muse.

Long ago, in what was then Malaya, when Burgess was trying to make English literature somehow real to his Malayan students, he formulated a theory that the Dark Lady of Shakespeare's imagination might really have been dark. That she might, in fact, have been African or Malayan—the presence of dark-skinned people being not unheard of in 17th-century seafaring Britain. Burgess wrote a wonderful novel on this premise, *Nothing Like the Sun*, in which the Dark Lady is a black woman whom Shakespeare loves, flees from and returns to, and who inspires his most intense creations from the early sonnets down to Cleopatra. She is, in effect, Will's Muse.

That's Enderby's idea, too, though his versions are far below his creator's. Instead of Burgess' careful mosaic of Elizabethan life, we get this sort of thing:

"Out in Silver Street, which the sun had promoted to gold, they saw beggars, limbless soldiers, drunken sailors, whores, dead cats, ordinary decent citizens in stuff gowns, a kilted Highlander with a flask of usquebaugh, in place of a sporran. A ballad singer with a few teeth sang"—and so on. Enderby's slack writing can't be blamed on Burgess, of course, except that Burgess's own is slack enough in this novel. It most comes to life with the entrance of April Elgar. She overawes the fools, entrances Enderby and seems to have occult sources of poetic utterance. She awakens Enderby's old powers and summons forth Burgess' best efforts. And, of course, that's as it should be.

But not only is Enderby disturbing Shakespeare's bones, two-timing him with the Dark Lady and pillaging his own creator's works; Enderby is himself being put to overtime by Burgess. He first appeared in *Inside Mr. Enderby* (1960), a rich and large comic character, whose self-involvement, grotesque cookery (wonderful and wonderfully horrible meals being a Burgess specialty of old) and genuine devotion to his Muse were all fully imagined. *Enderby Outside* (1967) was a little more rackety. But if these two were Parts

I and II of Burgess' own Falstaff epic, then *A Clockwork Testament* was decidedly *The Merry Wives of Windsor:* Enderby called back to suffer grotesque misadventures in New York, be humiliated over an improbable film project, and at last expire in a hotel room.

So that was the end of Enderby, except that it wasn't. Burgess has now recalled him from the grave. Now, somewhat unreal and incomplete, as befits a ghost, he is made to suffer grotesque misadventures in Indiana, be humiliated over an improbable stage production, and at last—well, he doesn't die. In the end of *Enderby's Dark Lady* we are offered a sort of science fiction (by Enderby) in which Shakespeare takes his revenge on those who disturb his bones—a joke that gets funnier the more you think about it.

In his introduction, Burgess offers some thoughts about how Hamlet and Don Quixote can never really die and how all fiction is a hypothesis. We didn't need that. He is perfectly free to reimagine Enderby. We only wish it were a better book, not so slapdash and unfelt. But if it falls among the lesser Burgesses and not the greater (the greatest being surely among the true achievements in fiction in the late 20th century), then it is better than no Burgess at all. That is a development we ought all to hope might be indefinitely postponed.

1984

LITTLE WILSON AND BIG GOD

In the winter of 1953, down with the mumps, the writer who would become Anthony Burgess spent six weeks typing out a short novel on a borrowed typewriter. He had written much poetry, but chiefly he thought of himself as a composer. Novel-writing he found absurdly easy in comparison to, say, writing a symphony: a monody, a concerto for solo flute.

Many years and many novels later, Anthony Burgess sat in the lobby of the Plaza Hotel with hours to wait before a plane flight. His best work, he thought, lay now in the past; American reviewers had not liked his last two novels; perhaps it was time to write no more (a hot wave of shame came to this reviewer's cheek to read this, for he has written dismissive things about *Enderby's Dark Lady* and *The Kingdom of the Wicked*). It seemed a time to begin an apologia, which is not an apology but an account. And two years later, here is *Little Wilson and Big God*, the first volume of Burgess's autobiography.

In the very first paragraph we find ourselves spoken to by a man who is patently modest and likable, playful and intelligent; less patently but no less certainly a writer of wonderful grace and fluidity:

"A Foreword to the reader is a hindword to an author. The author knows what has been written, the reader has yet to find out. The author...sometimes stands at the threshold which the foreword is, biting his nails and wondering whether a brief warning, an apology for inadequacy or excess, an avowal of mediocrity where he had intended brilliance, might not be a courteous gesture to the person who has had the kindness to at least pick up his book."

It can be safely predicted that few who pick up *Little Wilson and Big God* will wish to put it down again unfinished. It is being touted as better than his novels, praise which a novelist does not like to hear, and which is not so anyway; but it is a fine thing of its kind, a vivid recounting of a mostly unremarkable life (as of Volume One at least), generous toward an ungenerous world, and truffled with good jokes, good words, odd lore and odd people. It carries him (on his own back) through childhood and the Byzantine intricacies of a British schooling, through the War and his colonial experience, up to the point when, under what he thought was an imminent sentence of death, he began to write in earnest to provide for his prospective widow.

In his first pages Burgess suggests that he will probably write no more when the sequel to this volume is finished, that perhaps the critics are right who have said he has written too much already. We can only hope that remarks of this kind are like those remarks of really quite healthy elders that the grave calls to them, that soon they'll be out of everyone's way and no trouble any longer, and so on; remarks to be countered by cheerful encouragement and genuine expressions of affection. The list of his books is indeed long—two columns of tiny print at the beginning of this book—but to know that the last one had in fact appeared would be an occasion of very great sorrow indeed.

Anthony Burgess was born John Wilson, and his beginnings

were those he assigned to the heroine of *The Pianoplayers*: his father came home to Manchester from the Army at the end of the First World War to find John's mother and sister lying dead of influenza in bed together, and John hungry but alive in the crib nearby.

His father, a feckless dipsomaniac, easy-going and remote, never quite knew what to do with his son, and John, undersized and skinny, grew up without much affection from a stepmother and stepsisters. He seems to have been one of those who transmute an early lack of affection into a ceaseless appetite for sexual comfort later on. Fortunately, there seems to have been no lack of that. Boy and man, he was welcomed by women of many kinds and colors in many towns and lands, and toward all of them his respect and gratitude is still fresh. The load of Catholic guilt he says he long carried—Catholic guilt being chiefly a residue of sex, like soiled sheets—is less convincingly conveyed. Maybe it hasn't persisted as sharply.

The Protestant reformation never took as firm hold in the North of England as it did in the South, but Burgess's traditions are not those of the unworldly (and largely factitious) Old Catholic magnates of *Brideshead Revisited*; Burgess's roots are in Irish Manchester, a working-class city, where religion was a simple matter, a badge of difference dividing "cat licks" and "proddy dogs" into proud but not often violently contentious bands.

His faith was to become a more complex and demanding thing for Burgess. He has suffered from the bizarre conviction, common to so many intelligent ex-Catholics, that his old religion, while impossible to live within, has an impregnable logic about it, makes an intellectual sense that can never be confuted. Burgess's great hero, James Joyce, was once asked by a Protestant preacher if he would not, having apostatized, consider Methodism instead. Joyce replied that he had lost his faith, but he had not lost his mind.

Burgess might have remained stuck in that paradox had he not gone East to Malaya, and taught English among the several Malayan peoples and religions, the heat and the dark-skinned women. It put things in perspective, including his Catholic guilt. It also generated his first successful fiction—a trilogy about the end of British rule in Malaya, *The Long Day Wanes*—and planted the seeds of one of his finest novels, *Nothing Like the Sun*, all about guilty Shakespeare's obsession with a dark-skinned woman.

Burgess's novels have been so many, so generous in the amusements they offered, so easy to read and enjoy, that the subtlety of their crafting and the complex music of their narrative structures have often been overlooked. The one work of art we all construct is the story of our own past lives, and it is usually ill-told and self-serving; the great set-pieces in Burgess's account are the work of a novelist in command of considerable means.

There is, for example, the wonderfully dreary and Orwellian account of the war years which Burgess spent propagandizing for the British Way and Purpose, topped off with an appearance by Orwell himself, to whom Burgess suggests some details for his new book. There is the weird comedy of his early married life—his wife torn between two brothers, each of whom wants her to leave Burgess for himself, while Burgess looks on and drinks with all of them—which must have been more hurtful and confusing to him than he makes it seem to us. And Malaya at the setting of the sun on the Empire, both Burgess and his wife floating small adulteries on oceans of gin, is a small novel itself.

"Memories sometimes lie in relation to facts, but facts also lie in respect of memory," he writes, a sentence which deserves some parsing. I believe he has given himself the liberty of shaping his history, or rather denied himself the liberty of not shaping it. And I do not believe that his father ever really said, when his second wife complained of a 'orrible 'eadache, that what she needed was a couple of aspirates. That is a joke no one in this long and engaging story is quite capable of making except the author and hero himself.

1987

SOME OTHERS

The Arabian Nightmare
by Robert Irwin

*T*HERE ARE THOSE WHO at the breakfast table, or even the dinner table, are ready to recount their dreams in great detail; there are others, far rarer, who are willing to listen avidly, waiting perhaps for a revelation, a key, a lesson that could be learned no other way, or only for a frisson of the uncanny. They will particularly enjoy *The Arabian Nightmare*, though all are welcome to this witty and convoluted phantasmagoria.

On June 18, 1486 (an oddly exact date, considering what follows) a certain Balian of Norwich, pilgrim to the desert shrine of St. Catherine, enters Cairo, "puzzling at the many unexpected features of the city he saw on every side—the rugs spread out to display the little brass idols of Mahound, Apollyon and Tergavent, the twisted candy-columned doorways, the storks that nested in towers and minarets and drifted across the sky from one to another, the broad staircases that shot up steeply from the main highway closely lined with statues of elephants and men."

Cairo (this Cairo, at least) is one of those cities whose streets, seeming to lead outward, only circle back again. Balian intends to pass through Cairo, but stumbles instead into an interlocking nest of dreams from which he cannot exit. It may be that he is suffering from the Arabian Nightmare, which is going around (so he is led to believe): this horrid dream disorder condemns the sufferer to experience hours of hideous torment each night, hours that consume dream-years, dream-lifetimes of pain, but which he awakes from not aware that he has dreamed at all.

An Englishman who befriends the feckless Balian, Michael Vane, insists that he can only be treated for his dream disturbances by the greatest practitioner of dream medicine, the Father of Cats, who lives in Cairo under the protection of the Sultan (who has sleep problems of his own). The Father of Cats is a strangely modern practitioner, doing experimental brain surgery on his beloved cats; he has trained his agent Vane in all the arts of lucid dreaming, and given him a different view of dreaming from that held by the dull majority: "They visualize life and dream as containers, and they think either that the dream is locked within the casket of waking life or that waking life is locked inside the dream." The truth, says the Father of Cats, is otherwise.

From the Father of Cats, Balian hears of the nature of the Alam al-Mithal, which we might call Dreamland, though this Arabian version has none of the languor and sweetness of that word It is a quite dreadful place, many-leveled and peopled with malevolent creatures; it is, moreover, bent on invading waking life. Indeed, it may have already begun, and Balian may be its victim.

On the other hand, the sufferings of Balian may be inflicted on him not by the Nightmare but by the voice telling us his tale, which seems to be the voice of the marketplace storyteller, Dirty Yoll, he with the ape on his back. Yoll is anti-dream; dreams only make people want to sleep, he says, where stories make them want to wake up. Certainly Balian wants to wake up; but he is stuck in that sort of dream (there really is a Greek word for it) from which the dreamer dreams that he awakes, only to find (or lose) himself in a further dream.

In the Alam al-Mithal, says the Father of Cats, "there are more signs than meanings, and more causes than events," just as there are in this book. There are the Laughing Dervishes, who foretell the coming of the Fifth Messiah and the end of the world (four other Messiahs and four other ends of the world have already come and gone, but the world was too dull to notice them); there is Fatima the Deathly and her imaginary sister Zuleyka (or is it the other way around?). There are the Leper Knights of the Order of St. Lazarus, sworn enemies of Islam and the Father of Cats (or are they?), the man in the dirty turban, and the two dwarves, Barfi and Ladoo, who cannot always tell which of them is which. They are all, of course, connected with each other; they all appear several times and under conflicting aspects; the revolving events they cause or suffer keep seeming on the point of making some large and ghastly sense, only to slip again into a convincingly dreamlike oblivion: a restless incoherence, shadowed by ungraspable meaning.

Stories are the opposite of dreams, as Yoll insists, and yet when

The Arabian Nightmare *by Robert Irwin*

he attempts to tell a full-blown *Arabian Nights*-style story-within-a-story inside this dream, his story becomes infected too, and cannot redeem: it is pushed to parodically fatuous lengths in the way John Barth likes to do, and is not finally different from poor Balian's dream-inside-a-dream.

Dreams are endless and stories are circular, so the only way the book can be closed is with that phrase so many schoolboy writers have used when they have got themselves entangled in some impossible tissue of fantasy: *Then he woke up.* Which is just what Irwin resorts to, with one last and perhaps inevitable claustrophobic twist.

This is the sort of book that is often easier to write than to read, but Irwin keeps the miasmic pot boiling with verve. As with all the great "Oriental" tall-tale-tellers from Sir John Mandeville to Borges, it's impossible to tell where the real erudition ends and the imaginary begins (part of the fun, of course). The Nightmare itself is a conceit worthy of Borges, an unspeakable disease which the sufferer does not know he suffers from, whose existence is therefore impossible to prove. In Borges' austere and minimal telling it would have haunted the reader's days for a lifetime; Irwin's language is a sort of lively and unexceptionable Standard Modern, but not quite memorable enough to cause the reader, when he at last awakes (I mean puts down the book) to be unable to forget the dream.

1987

The Young Visiters: Or, Mr Salteena's Plan by Daisy Ashford

Sometime around 1890, a nine-year-old English girl named Daisy Ashford, who had apparently been spending the same number of hours inside grown-up novels as nine year-olds today spend watching TV, sat down to write a novel of her own. The result was *The Young Visiters* (the spelling is Miss Ashford's, as is the creative spelling throughout her book). It first made its way into print in 1919, but has not been available for many years in this country; now here it is again, just in time to stuff stockings or seal friendships as it once did.

Like all good Victorian novels, this one's about love, money, and class, and it's more frank and less fooled about them than most. Mr. Salteena, "an elderly man of 42," confesses "I am not quite a gentleman but you would hardly notice it but can't be helped anyhow." His ward, Ethel Monticue (you must have a young ward in such a story) falls for Mr. Salteena's friend Bernard, and Bernard volunteers to help Mr. Salteena become "more seemly"—which involves paying for lessons in gentlemanliness from Bernard's friend the Earl of Clincham, who lives in the Crystal Palace:

"You see these compartments are the haunts of the Aristockracy said the earl and they are kept going by peaple who have got something funny in their family and who want to be less mere if you can comprehend." Indeed Mr. Salteena can, and gladly pays up.

How Bernard and Ethel break Mr. Salteena's heart (for of course he was in love with her himself); how Mr. Salteena gets smuggled into a royal levée by the wonderfully worldly Earl; how Bernard proposes marriage ("Let us now bask under the spreading trees said Bernard in a passiunate tone"): every scene, every effect she attempts, this astonishing writer achieves; she manages a ball, a wedding, a party, each with its grand and its intimate moments, its revelations and reverses, with the aplomb of a Virginia Woolf or a Jane Austen, and all in a hundred small pages.

Daisy Ashford has that cruel honesty which comes with a child's total acceptance of her society's rules. She understands that the good life must be paid for: "Costly" and "sumpshius" are favorite adjectives. Her happy ending is very qualified: Mr. Salteena becomes a gentleman, "galloping madly after the Royal Carrage," but has to marry a nobody "who was a bit annoying at times especially when he took to dreaming of Ethel and wishing he could have married her."

For obvious reasons, literary prodigies are rarer than musical ones; writers have to have lived. But for *The Young Visiters* and its author the only adjective is "Mozartian."

1991

~≈~ Labrador BY KATHRYN DAVIS ~≈~

*T*HE PROLOGUE OF Kathryn Davis's first novel is as charged with wonder and as flagrantly skillful as a fire-eater's act. A person named Rogni is speaking, telling of the Nurse-of-becoming, at work in her house in a far northern landscape, imagining two sisters: "This old woman was greedy and filled with rapture at the prospect of seeing them rise from the steam of her teapot, and she thought about how she would take them, like damp and rumpled handkerchiefs, and shake them out into the little lace-edged things that they were—Willie a rectangle, Kathleen a circle—and hang them over the cookstove to dry." But she lets the sisters burn, and blows the black pieces everywhere. "In the beginning, this is how it was."

The first pages of the story that follows only deepen and broaden the fabulation. Now the voice speaking is Kathleen's, the younger of two American sisters growing up in New England in the 1950s. She addresses her older sister, the first person she loved, whom she still loves obsessively:

"Into my eye, Willie. A fleck of you flew in there, making a tear well up—that little shining star you saw and swept onto the tip of your finger to suck. It fell and fell down the dark shaft of your throat, trickling into your heart, where it glowed. The room filled with light."

So hopeful and compelling is this inception that the reader's momentum carries him through many further pages without reservation. Reservations must eventually be felt, but this brief, passionate novel continues to compel the attention to the end.

Willie is the intensely imaginative, the febrile and dangerous sister, who will eventually go a little mad; but her sister Kathleen has an accompanying angel. Not a guardian angel, for he seems incapable of helping her much, and in fact will for a time betray her; he is a distant cousin of those feckless angels of old movies who have a hard time grasping the exigencies of human life. He is the Rogni who begins this story, and he punctuates it with other tales that tell of Willie and Kitty in variously reversed, transfigured or inverted forms. Kitty is the only one who can see him and converse with him, but it is Willie whom Rogni comes to love—and desire.

Willie grows into a steady contempt for her parents—she calls them Mr. Noodle and the Mouse Queen—and they are indeed two damp souls, at once cold and anxious for love. She studies ballet, she engineers a romance with an older man, a gentle mystic named Peter Mygatz. While she is busy with these things, Kitty is busy with nothing but her thoughtlessly sadistic sister: trying to be noticed by her, trying to spy on her and Peter in his trailer, trying to win her love.

Kitty's release comes out of a family myth: her grandfather who long ago went off to Labrador to live with an Indian woman. He reappears, and Kathleen gives him a share of her jealous heart; she goes with him on a journey to Labrador, the geographical center of the book.

The web of symbol in which the slight action of *Labrador* is caught wraps more tightly with every page. The grandfather is not different from the white bear whom Kitty dreams of, the bear who kills him. Bella, the old Indian woman jealous of Kitty's intrusion into her Labrador *ménage*, is also the Nurse-of-becoming, lover of the King of the Bears. The angel Rogni is sexuality itself, and identical with Peter Mygatz; despite Willie's confession, Kitty is certain that it is not Peter but Rogni himself who has impregnated Willie at the book's conclusion.

The web is intensified beyond coherence by Rogni's interpolated tales, which are decked with the stuffs of meaning, but seem not to mean: one sounds like a folk tale, another a Dinesen-like Gothic tale, and none are like real stories at all. "Angels are avid for their stories to have endings," Kitty comes to learn. "But it is also true that as storytellers they are unencumbered by the idea of motivation."

In that sense, Kitty's story-telling—and Davis's—are angelic: *Labrador* generates, despite the unintelligibility of certain of its narrative turns, and the skein of metaphoric doubling they are bound in, an undoubted urgency, driving toward an ending which, though we are not allowed to imagine what sort of ever-after it points to, is apparently a happy one.

    Kathryn Davis has taken the sad and binding stuff of many a first novel—the inescapable family, the growth into knowledge, the heavy impermeability of matter and the queasy processes of becoming—and fashioned genuinely new embodiments for it. When she looks back at this book after completing her third or fourth or eighth or tenth, there will doubtlessly be things she will wish to undo. She may well wince at the wholly incredible comic Irish maid, a far more unlikely character than the angel Rogni. She will have learned by then that when she has made a sentence do two lovely tricks, she should not insist it do a third, and then take a bow as well. She will also have much reason for pride. I think *Labrador* will still be worth reading.

1988

~ Pinto and Sons by Leslie Epstein ~

Science fiction is common; fiction about science is much rarer. Leslie Epstein's *Pinto and Sons* makes science—the scientific method, the possibilities of technology based on science—the governing metaphor of a greathearted saga of ambition, hope, and loss.

Adolf Pinto, Epstein's Quixotic hero, is a lanky Hungarian Jew who in 1847 is studying medicine in Boston, sent over by his family, soap-manufacturers of Pressburg. A. Pinto (as he generally refers to himself) is a fit hero for the picaresque he must act out: naive, optimistic, full of boundless energy and an apparently iron physique. In the opening pages he sits spellbound in an operating theater watching the first use of ether in an operation. It works! Life without pain!

Having seen Science triumph over suffering, Pinto is appalled to learn that its inventor intends to keep the manufacturing process to himself, and make millions on the patent. In conjunction with other medical students whose later history will be bound up with his own—Matt Cole, Frank Townsend—Pinto works out the secret of the process. They try out Pinto's recipe on the Cole family dog, who sleeps through an extraordinary maiming as the students, high on the escaped fumes of their own concoction, slice away in triumph. The dog too (it is that kind of book) will play a further part in Pinto's destiny.

Through a series of mishaps, Pinto loses his chance to provide ether free to the world: just as he will lose other chances, to cure an incurable disease, to make war obsolete. For Pinto is as luckless as he is brilliant, and his achievements and inspirations come always too early or too late, knocked aside by the bounding history of his times.

He goes West (by mistake) in the mad rush for gold that draws his medical-student chums as well. He fails to find gold, and sets up as a merchant instead; but Townsend and Cole, having foolishly bought a seeded claim, turn it into a paying mine—a high-tech installation burrowing hundreds of feet downward along a vein of ore-bearing quartz.

The Neptune Mine, a miracle of technology at the service of greed, is a wonderful construction, illustrating that law of fiction by which horrors can be made exhilarating simply by the energy and vividness of their description. The mine, penetrating the young California earth into lava-heated regions, grows so hot that no white miner can stand it; but the Modoc Indians who have lived over the lava fields for centuries turn out to be extraordinarily immune to heat. When the mine reaches depths of half a mile and more, a ventilation shaft is dug alongside it, and a vast sail constructed to drive the desert wind downward and cool the mine. Then ice is cut from a far-off glacier and rolled across the desert on logs, so that the sail-wind passing over it will air-condition the shaft. Then . . . but the Neptune mine, a sort of reverse Babel overreaching downwards rather than upwards, will have a Babel-like fate as well, and Frank Townsend, like Mistah Kurtz in *Heart of Darkness*, will descend into depths of another kind, to become the mad idol of the Modocs he has oppressed.

It is the sons of these Modoc miners who are the "sons" of the book's title: young boys strangely eager for learning, which Pinto happily supplies. He teaches them English from the poems of Burns, his only volume, and from then on they speak in Highland accents and sentiments ("We dinna be ghosts, Mister-r-r Pinto:" it is also that kind of book). He dresses them in top hats and striped pants like Etonians and inducts them into the religion of Science. The other Modocs have been given white nicknames—Gentleman Jack, Two-toes Tom, One-eyed Mose—and so Pinto gives his boys, the Heirs of Galileo, the Disciples of Bacon, their own nicknames: Newton Mike, Kepler Jim, Humboldt Johnny. Together they embark on the next great aborted Pinto achievement: the discovery of a cure for rabies.

Only lengthy quotation would do justice to the hilarity, the excitement, the passion of this enterprise, conducted on a hidden level of the Neptune Mine even as the mine reaches toward the one-mile level. The Cole family dog is part of it, and so is the *idiot-savant* child that Pinto has fathered on a Modoc woman.

Pinto and Sons *by Leslie Epstein*

With the frustration of Pinto's hopes, and the end of the hellish mine, the story, which has been drastic but largely comical, turns dark. The final third of the book, in which the Modocs dance back their dead from the mine's depths and turn against the whites who have used and cheated them, is based on the actual history of the Modoc War; as death and treachery multiply, Pinto's faith in reason and science seem ever more misplaced, and his inventive energy only makes the war more terrible. We are reminded that Epstein is the author of a classic novel of the Holocaust, *The King of the Jews*.

The great suspense of a book like this—greater than any surprise of the plot—is whether the writer can sustain its wild career to the end. In later chapters, the writer's choices begin to seem somewhat arbitrary; a sense of authorial *triage*—who will live, who will die— sets in, and our sympathies have been largely sapped just short of the end. That's inevitable, probably, in such a book. No matter: *Pinto and Sons* is a fantastic epic of the heroic age of applied science, a fit book to put on the shelf with the great tall tales of American expansion—*Roughing It, Little Big Man, The Sot-weed Factor*— books that express in their very unlikelihood and careening exaggeration an essential truth about our unlikely history.

1990

IN THE BEAUTY OF THE LILIES
BY JOHN UPDIKE

*T*HE NOVEL, SINCE ITS beginnings, has generated large numbers of subgenres, dividing itself into further and further small pieces to please segments of the reading public. The varieties have lately seemed to proliferate wildly, like varieties of snack foods proliferating on the supermarket shelves, and the bright if somewhat illusory array attracts not only readers but writers tempted to try something new, to see if they can turn out a campus farce, or an alternative-history novel, or a techno-thriller, or all three in one.

The kind that has attracted John Updike's restless talent is the one where the generations of a family experience all the currents and counter-currents of the century, which variously pass them by, destroy them, or carry them to fame and adventure, thence to disillusion and loss. Among the usual components of this popular flavor are evocative lists of pop-culture icons, walk-ons by real historical characters, and family members who recapitulate the experiences of earlier members in changed circumstances. All are present in Updike's version; so are Updike's voice and his repertoire of gesture and feeling, as distinctively his as the genre he is working in is common property.

Two themes connect the generations of the Wilmot family as they successively appear before us: one is God, the other is the movies. On a summer afternoon in 1910, in his nice parsonage in Paterson, New Jersey, the Reverend Clarence Arthur Wilmot all at once loses his faith in God; in the darkened nickelodeons of the city, he finds all that he will ever know of transcendence.

Clarence has at least the courage of his unbelief. He gives up his comfortable living, reducing his family to poverty, and tries to make money selling encyclopedias to the working people of Paterson, most of whom are worse off than himself because of the long Paterson silk strike of 1913 (the one that broke the power of the

Wobblies). His decline in status (and subsequent sickness and early death) has various effects on his family. His wife Stella will forget, and remake her husband into a sort of martyr, too good for the world, but she will never be entirely able to forgive. His son Jared's natural cynicism will find fuel in his father's foolish abnegation. And his youngest son Teddy will never forgive God, for not relenting and giving his father the slightest sign of his existence.

For Clarence and his crisis of faith, Updike employs an upholstered prose, cut from that heavy gabardine yardage that runs from say George Eliot to William Dean Howells: "As, with an expression of morose benignity, he sat consuming his share of the pork roast and its ample vegetable accompaniment, his wife and children—except for the youngest, little careful tonge-tied Teddy—were exceptionally animated and conversational." Only when he drops it, in Teddy's section, do we realize (gratefully) that this orotundity will not be permanent; we have already been reminded why the manner was discarded.

The world picks up speed dangerously in the 1920s, and frightens Teddy into abnegations of his own. His greatest skill—one he will pass on to his own grandson in malignant form—is for avoidance, observation, and safety, and it will build him a small and, as he sees it in old age, an almost perfectly satisfactory life: he has avoided all the shoals upon which others have foundered. Not only that, he has known real love (with Emily, who has a malformed foot and a careful privacy of her own because of it) and has had a job he never tires of, as a postman in a small Delaware town.

The people in novels such as this one are always more aware of their historical moment and its signposts than are people in other novels. "Gangsters were killing each other, and people were doing dance marathons, and the German mark was worth four trillion to the dollar. Wilson must have been right: the Allies should have been nicer to the Germans." These commonplaces about the way of the world may simply reflect the commonplace minds of the characters, but there are a lot of them, and many seem to be the author's own shorthand; too many sentences sound like they could have come from almost any book of the genre: "She was drifting on America's sea of appetites and easy money and jazz." "Now came a time of changes and decisions, events that tumbled together confusedly in the family memory—a quick avalanche settling into the static decade of the Depression."

The difficulty is that we know this story, both as fact and as fiction, and within it the characters mostly do and feel about what we expect them to do and feel; amazing and startling as it all must have been to live through, in this kind of recounting it takes on a melancholy inevitability. Never less than engaging, the book often threatens to become a page-turner in a less than flattering sense. What continually saves it is Updike's astonishing ability to reproduce sensory experience: kisses, or sunlight on snow, or "the day's buzzing impervious beauty, with the distant cows on the world's edge and the soft steady chunk of oars coming from far in the other direction," or New York pigeons on a ledge "rotating in their drying offal, leaking a throbbing noise out of their gray rainbow throats"—something surprising on nearly every page, as surprising as the encounters with Our Times are predictable.

Teddy too goes to the movies, but they somewhat frighten him with their extremities of pain and urgency, even the comedies. What lifted his father from the anguish of non-being and the pointless suffering of existence only remind Teddy of them the more intensely. But for Teddy and Emily's daughter Essie, growing up in the '40s, movies are not an escape; real life is the movies, and life itself the imitation. For Essie, Updike adopts a swift style richer than anything that has come before, and his vivid evocations of the artificial life of the screen, appealing and vivid throughout, now come through Essie's consciousness: "She [Ginger Rogers] wore dresses that were mountains of ruffles and big snakes of ostric feathers that came up and covered her chin and no matter how fast he was making her move and twirl on the slippery ballroom floor her eyes stayed level and calm and warm like lamps lit inside her head."

Essie, remade as Alma DeMott, will herself enter alive into that empyrean as a star; single-minded and heroically self-regarding, she is also the only one of the Wilmots who genuinely and spontaneously believes in God: not in church or religion, certainly not in sin or hell, but in God as the source of the universe's love and beneficence just for her. God catches up her son Clark in the final part, and destroys him; but we never know that Clark really believes in anything.

A cliché who understands he is a cliché (the useless and

insufficiently loved son of beautiful remote mother and her succession of nonentity husbands,) Clark in 1990 is in his twenties, working at a ski resort which his great-uncle Jared has made out of a played-out copper mountain in Colorado. Teddy's talent for evasion and Jared's cynicism, his own rootlessness and irreality (movies are the realest thing in his life too, but he no longer believes in them) add up in Clark to a plain zero; when a casual pickup takes him to a commune in the mountains run by a religious zealot, the leader "stepped into him like a drifter taking over an empty shack."

With prophet Jesse and his Temple we are in purlieus that seem more remote from Updike's own growing-up even than Paterson in 1913, and yet are as sensually sharp and exact as anything in the book, a physical environment of astonishing verisimilitude, the "mummified bundles of guns smelling of the oil that kept them eternally young," the barrel of the gun assigned to Clark that "floated outward like a flexible, sensitive wand when he embraced the polished stock, of silky checkered walnut."

The outcome is clear early on, and it is to be wondered what exactly we are to make of the Waco-in-an-alternative-universe that ends the book abruptly. The mechanisms of apocalyptic belief are not studied, as we never learn that Clark actually believes; Jesse, the self-taught zealot, is a sort of cliché too, with his endless askew Biblical references, his clutch of young wives, his prophecies of destruction. The whammies (as the movie-makers of Clark's generation call them) come as expected, and are a *tour de force* of narrative management, though we can sometimes glimpse the author busy at work consulting his gun digests and reference works (*Mad Man In Waco* and *Religious Cults in America* are mentioned in the author's Afterword).

The key to Updike's intent may lie in the epigraph from which the otherwise puzzling title comes: As He died to make men holy, the Hymn says, let us die to make men free. The God that Clarence Wilmot abandoned at such cost seizes upon his great-grandson, but—very nearly too late—Clark is given the chance to die in making at least a few women and children free. It remains a question what, when we awaken both from the dream of Revelation and the revelations in the darkened theater, we awaken to.

1996

~ Story of O by Pauline Reage ~

STORY OF O (note the lack of an article, consistent with the French title, *Histoire d'O*) appeared in 1965 from Grove Press, that fabulous font of the odd and the dark from around the world. I couldn't afford that edition; I had (and still have; it is—as they say—beside me as I write) the Black Cat paperback, $1.95, with its all-white cover and black type title, and that name, Pauline Réage, which even to my all-American eye seemed like a mask, a black cat mask. There was speculation at the time, I shared it, that the real author had to be a man; but a woman friend of mine said no, only a woman could think of things so cruel. (What had she herself thought of?) The world in which the book came to me was rapidly changing; sex had just been invented and was believed to be a liberation, a realm of guiltless and childlike delight, sunlit. I thought that. And then there came this book, from somewhere sunless and *profonde*, so fierce and so dark. Not only was it about slavery and humiliation rather than freedom and fun; it was powered by a current which André Pieyre de Mandiargues said in one of the book's several prefaces "comes from the soul and not from the body, and which in fact is directed against the body." How can limitless sex be directed against the body? I didn't know, then. But the book almost burned me to hold: as Réage says of what O has done, "even when it merely occurred in thought, a cape of fire, a burning breastplate extending from the shoulders to the knees, descended upon her." "Limitless" was going to turn out to be a word of awful ambiguity: this also we didn't know, then; but we would learn.

2000

Hermit in Paris by Italo Calvino, Translated by Martin McLaughlin

In her preface to this collection of her husband's autobiographical writings, journals and interviews, Esther Calvino remembers suggesting to Calvino that he return to writing *The Road to San Giovanni*, his autobiography. Calvino refused: "Because my biography is not yet . . ." He didn't complete the thought. Not yet finished? An autobiography by definition leaves out one key moment in a life, and Calvino might have been thinking of a way he might wait to experience that moment before completing his own. In a Calvino story or novel, it would certainly have been possible.

Instead, we have this collection, which his wife found after his death gathered in a folder and annotated by Calvino with dates of publication. These are presented here in the order in which they appeared in print. The collection also includes a diary of his trip to America in 1959–60, in the form of letters to a friend at the Turin publishing house Einaudi where Calvino was an editor. Calvino was inclined to publish this diary as a book, the title of which was to be *An Optimist in America*, but decided it was too slight; it is the centerpiece of this volume, the longest and certainly to Americans the most interesting. The title of this volume, *A Hermit in Paris*, comes from a very late piece in which Calvino describes his life as an outsider in Paris: odd, because the bulk of the volume describes his childhood, coming-of-age, and maturity as an Italian and an Italian writer in Italy.

Italo Calvino's work is unique in the literature of the 20th century; it would be impertinent in this brief notice to try to characterize it, since almost anything said about *Cosmicomics* or *Invisible Cities* or *Mister Palomar* wouldn't apply to any of the other works. In a 1978 piece, Calvino addresses this from the maker's point of view: "Writing is such a boring and solitary occupation; if you repeat yourself an infinite sadness seizes hold of you." Not of most writers, actually; but it may be the reason for what Calvino calls with (false) modesty "that collection of fragments that is my *ouevre*."

Calvino's self-revelation in these pieces is delicate, frank yet circumspect, and entirely winning. He grew up in rural Italy the children of left-wing agricultural experts, humanist and nonreligious, who were imprisoned and pestered by the Fascists; he himself became a partisan at the end of the war and a Communist afterwards (many of the pieces here included recount these facts and their implications, to interestingly different effect as Calvino gets older). He broke with the Party after the Hungarian uprising of 1956, and thereafter grew more and more apolitical. The moral purpose, worthwhile work, and humane vision he ceased to find in political programs he found, somewhat reluctantly, only in writing.

In the American diary, though, we have Calvino not as a mature skeptic but a younger optimist, who wanders the huge country he has of course known about and read about all his life (he went fishing with Hemingway in Italy in 1948!), becoming or revealing himself in the process to be—what else?—a Calvino character. "In America *all* the cars are enormous... I am tempted to hire immediately an enormous car, not even to drive it, just for the psychological sense of being in control of the city." "The beatniks naturally fraternize with [Calvino's traveling companion, Spanish writer Fernando] Arrabal, who is also bearded... [Allen] Ginsberg lives with another bearded man as man and wife and would like Arrabal to be present at their bearded couplings." He visits at Sarah Lawrence: "Girls in trousers and big socks and multicolored jerseys, just like in films about college life, flutter down from the buildings where they have their faculty rooms and dormitories. Lunch is very meagre because in any case the girls want to keep their figure (while the starving tutors protest)." In class they discuss *The Brothers Karamazov*, "but these young girls are surely as far from Dostoevsky as the moon. Seeing Dostoevsky and Russian religious thought skimming over that gathering of young heiresses in Westchester brings on the kind of astonishment and enthusiasm that would be provoked by a collision of planets."

Astonishment and enthusiasm—mild and wise—characterize the piece, as they do Calvino's later imaginary journeys through space and time. Even the commonplaces of his encounters with

America from New York to Los Angeles are fresh; he has what Samuel Johnson called the necessary quality of a good traveler, the "willingness to be pleased." In California, "All the systems to help traffic flow work with miraculous speed: one night in San Francisco coming back from a party with a friend a little bit merry, the car ended up stranded, off the road; it was raining, we ran to a public telephone to call the emergency services, and we had not even got back to the car but the lorry was already there pulling the car out." Stopped by a cop in LA apparently for being a pedestrian in a city without them—actually for jaywalking, a non-Italian concept—Calvino sees that in fact pedestrians are protected by law: "Since they are few in number, like the redskins, they are trying to preserve them."

I do not have the Italian version of the book and am not at all competent to judge the translation, but it seems a bit erratic; I kept trying to guess just exactly what English phrase the translator had reached for and missed—that "in any case" in the account of the college lunch was surely supposed to be "above all"? What could be meant by "ruthless trouble-spots" in the Italian war? A "lynch squad" ought of course to be a "lynch mob." And so on. Never mind: This brief book, engaging for students of Calvino and interesting for all, is indispensable for his account of a moment in America. Our thanks are owed to Esther Calvino for including it.

2003

Adventures of the Artficial Woman by Thomas Berger

THOMAS BERGER, AS everyone knows, is the author of *Little Big Man*, one of the classic American tall tales. Before that book came the Reinhardt series of comic novels, and after his Cinderella moment, he returned to crafting a large number of highly individual but less widely read (or "midlist") novels, including such oddities as a revisionist and "ribald" retelling of the King Arthur legends (*Arthur Rex*); a *noir* private-eye novel, in which everyone speaks with an unlikely Henry James precision (*Who is Teddy Villanova?*); and *Regiment of Women*, a wonderfully extravagant philosophical romance in which men and women have changed roles in a future America—the men are made to wear dresses and elaborate underwear and makeup, and be secretaries and housewives, and the women are the bosses in suits and pasted-on moustaches.

Such a long career has to be viewed as a whole for any proper assessment, and every writer knows his latest (or last) novel may not be his best. Ah well—there's no putting it off any longer with these prefatory observations—*The Adventures of the Artificial Woman* is a remarkably poor book. As the perfunctory title announces, it's about an artificial woman—a robot, made by hand and in secret by Ellery Pierce, a "technician" working for a firm that makes animatronic creatures for theme parks—and her comic/satiric adventures among the flesh-and-blood. Phyllis, as her creator dubs her, is perfect in every way, exquisitely beautiful, indistinguishable from a human person, able to hold long conversations with her maker, and in the end capable of such autonomous actions as forging a career as a movie star and eventually being elected President. (Yes, it's the kind of book where an artificial human does things more efficiently than the emotional, foolish and needy real ones.)

It's apparent from the beginning that this isn't science fiction—

Adventures of the Artificial Woman by Thomas Berger

Richard Powers's *Galatea 2.2* is the book to read for a human/computerized female interaction that's equal to the paradoxes and problems involved. Berger has other fish to fry. Phyllis gets away from Ellery, and goes off on her own. She quickly discovers how to make a living in the sex trade, stripping, lap-dancing and phone sex, the comedy arising of course from her perfection as a sex object and her misunderstandings of male sexual needs and wants. From there she progresses to starring in a rather unlikely semi-pro production of *Macbeth*, which she turns into a big hit by introducing sex scenes. Her theater career leads to the movies, in which she stars as a super-heroine in a tight costume, doing her own stunts.

All of this behavior, or the possibility of developing it, is posited as arising from a "compact computer" inside Phyllis, but her adventures are really the immemorial ones of an outsider or Fool in human society, who succeeds precisely because she *doesn't* understand what's up, and proffers ambiguous messages for others to decode by wishful thinking (Jerzy Kosinski's Chance, in *Being There*, is an example). Much supposed humor derives from the way Phyllis responds to metaphors and figures of speech literally, and brightly answers rhetorical questions—what might be called the Amelia Bedelia effect, but which is also an ancient wheeze. Even this slight connection to the original premise is largely abandoned, however, as Phyllis moves from fading movie star to political candidate (succeeding, of course, because she takes no position on anything) and begins to talk like a modern Machiavelli whose only connection to robotics is her lack of sympathy with human feelings.

In its political burlesque, the book truly hits bottom. The loutish, priapic, hillbillyish (but secretly cunning and devious) President whom Phyllis defeats is left over from a previous age of satire; the idea that any presidential campaign will turn on empty showmanship and inconsequential promises might have been funny a very long time ago; the idea that the Vice President is a total nobody plucked from obscurity (here, a pharmacist met casually on the campaign trail) goes back to Kauffman and Ryskind's *Of Thee I Sing* (1931) and before. Nothing that anyone, including the robots, does or says is within the realm of even farcical possibility. Throughout there is Berger's patented oddity—that everybody speaks in the most artificial and preciously exact way. I laughed just once in the course of reading this book, when Pierce Ellery, now President Phyllis's advisor or stooge, cautions against her plan of installing a Mafia *capo* as head of the FBI (because who would know crime and criminals better?) "'Surely [Ellery responds] you aren't referring to the infamous Mafioso, head of the Spadini crime family? I assume you mean a respectable man of the same name. But is it advisable to encourage such a confusion?'"

Well, maybe I was tired. *The Adventures of the Artificial Woman* is not only about an animatronic robot, it reads rather as though it were written by one. It can't really harm Thomas Berger's large achievement as a steadily practicing writer of handmade novels in an age that doesn't treat such beings very kindly, but it does not add a cubit to his stature either.

2004

~ Being Dead by Jim Crace ~

*T*HE ENGLISH WRITER Jim Crace is a literary meteor. The jacket of his new novel carries praise that even in this age of blurb stagflation is impressive, and the inside flap lists many prizes and awards he has garnered since his first book. And indeed on the evidence of *Being Dead*, Crace is an extravagantly gifted writer unlike anyone else I can think of, and his new book a rare interleaving of writerly panache and common human feeling.

Joseph and Celice, two aging field biologists (Crace calls them "zoologists;" I think that term is antique, which doesn't mean it's used here in error), have returned to the strip of beach where they first met as doctoral students thirty-some years before. Here they first made love; and here, in the process of doing so again, they are brutally and senselessly murdered by a psychopathic thief. Their half-naked bodies go undiscovered in the dunes for many days, and the process of their corruption and dissolution is delicately and even winningly described, in short chapters that alternate with chapters telling of how they met, and how they first made love on that morning long ago. Later chapters add one further character: their daughter Syl, who has the task of finding them when they are at last discovered to be lost, and who is herself already lost to them, and perhaps to herself as well.

So the book announces itself as resembling the old practice of "quivering" the dead, a kind of wake in which the guests stand around the dead one's house and bed, making noise, shaking their quiver-sticks until the whole house rattles "as if a thousand crows were pecking at the roof," while reminiscing about the dead one, from old age back to childhood. "Their memories, exposed to the backward-running time of *quiverings* in which regrets became prospects, resentments became love, experience became hope, would up-end the hour-glass of Celice and Joseph's life together and let the sands reverse."

Except that as far as I know there is no such old practice; it's Crace's invention, part of the world he's making and inveigling us into by his nearly hypnotic word-spinning. Yet in his world as in ours, there is no resurrection but in memory and imagination; otherwise only the "everending [sic] days of being dead." There is chance and struggle and misfortune, hope defeated and abandoned, love holding on as best it can, and disappointment that kills or doesn't kill. There is the flesh, and its irremediable recycling by death, which is life too. Joseph and Celice both knew about that, they even celebrated it in their work, and they undergo it (of course) without reproach or complaint. Crace describes minutely the discolorations and dehydrations, the secretions and excretions of the process, as well as the progressive depredations of the crabs, the swag-flies, the squadron ants in the lissom grass, and the hispid buzzards overhead.

Except that in my dictionaries "squadron ants", "lissom grass", and "hispid buzzards" have no place; they are also, I must assume, Crace's inventions. Not that we don't have their equivalents in our world, with their own Latin names and gruesome ethologies. It's just that these are Crace's own.

There are writers who, abashed or self-conscious maybe, or highly sensitive to the boundary between life and art, will not set even a realistic story in our common geography, or name our cities and states in their books. Crace's story is set on Baritone Bay (named for the singing sands) in an unnamed coastal country, not necessarily England. Some writers can't admit brand names or common commercial products into their pages, but make up their own, like Crace's Eden pills; a drug, or gleewater, a drink. But I've never come on one outside the realms of faerie who chooses to make up his own everyday flora and fauna. Crace's selective inventiveness, his continuous little surprises, weave a delicate comedy around the grim matter of decay and loss that he purveys; you would say that by his art these things are redeemed, if Crace were not so clear that they aren't, and can't be.

Alerted to his methods, we notice more things. Is it intentional how much of the writing can be read as iambics? Syl, after her parents have been discovered, sits on the steps of a church and listens to the hymns, "as thin as water, and as nourishing." Am I imagining it, or are the sentences in which Crace dismisses these hymns written in hymn meter themselves: "Love songs transcend, transport, because there's such a thing as love. But hymns and prayers have feeble tunes because there are no gods."

We might call Crace a writer's writer, if what we mean by that often back-handed compliment is that a large part of the interest of his book lies in our fascination with his, Crace's, adventure in imagining and creating it, in getting safely to the shore of the last page after his *grand tour de force*. There is that fascination here. There is also much that is deeply moving about the absolutely common dilemma of Joseph, Celice and their daughter, of death and survival; it touches, and that is the writer's work too.

2000

~ The Fermata by Nicholson Baker ~

Late in Nicholson Baker's new novel, which is an allegory of pornography and its uses, and also contains a lot of pornography as well, a woman asks our hero, Arno Strine—or rather is imagined by him to be asking—a question that seems to puzzle many women about men's magazines: "All the women look the same. Why do men need so many identical pictures in one month?"

"In general [he imagines replying] men do want the same thing over and over. Different woman identically posed is the only difference they need. I would tell her that each tiny variation between two women's bodies constituted a huge difference from a sexual point of view... I would tell her this not as if I was pleased about it, but as if it were simply the way it was."

There is no doubt that for most men (anecdotal evidence suggests it is far less so for women) the eye is the supreme erotic organ. Men seem to carry within themselves a complex and variable template of what is sexually appealing, and their eyes are forever making fine discriminations—some eyes make finer discriminations than others—concerning the real women they see and how closely they approximate the template, which cannot itself actually be perceived except in the keenness of feeling aroused by such approximations; and none of this, template, search, feeling, seems to be any choice of theirs, but to be a fact of their biology.

Arno Strine, Baker's mild-mannered protagonist, an office temp in his thirties, is at once a questing hero of this male erotic eye, and at the same time much more familiar than most men are with the actualities of women's real bodies. Arno Strine has, intermittently, the ability to stop time: to make everything in (his? our? the?) universe come to a stop, while he alone moves and acts. He uses his talent not to become rich or powerful or for any purpose at all

The Fermata *by Nicholson Baker*

except to take women's clothes off and look at them—and sometimes touch them lightly.

He always restores their clothes as exactly as he can, so so that when he starts time up again they notice nothing. For them, no time has passed. Sometimes Strine allows himself to affect their lives or attempt to stir their feelings in small ways. This is the central premise and nearly the entire action of his profoundly strange book, except for some pornographic interludes written or imagined by Strine.

Now one of the things that overreaching artists do is to see how much can be made out of very little—an immense novel, say, made out of one ordinary day in Dublin. Baker has with great nerve taken up a fantasy that might fill a not very imaginative adolescent's horny half-hour, and not only made a novel out of it, but made a brilliantly, even euphorically successful one.

Nicholson Baker is the author of *Vox*, which was among other wonderful things a spirited defense of pornography, dirty talk and long-distance sex that ought to be read by everyone who thinks pornography is inevitably degrading to women and to the men who use it. Arno Strine is himself intensely and even sometimes uncomfortably aware of the moral ambiguities of his private, full-color, warm and living cheesecake: but he remains convinced that he has done the women he undresses no harm. They know nothing of his passage through their lives and their clothes, and anyway he has only the fondest, warmest feelings for them.

And yet when he tries to explain his actions (couched as mere hypotheses) to the one woman in the book with whom he has an ordinary real-time relationship, she finds the idea creepy and affronting, and actually breaks up with him when she suspects him of fantasizing about using her when she's not aware of it. He's not, of course, fantasizing.

Arno is a committed masturbator, who takes endless and giddy delight in retailing the minutest details of his semi-solitary adventures. He also rejoices in the details of the bizarre means he has found for entering what he calls *fermata* (in music, the holding or sustaining of a tone), and these often sound like the complicated private spells that schizophrenics use to keep their invisible enemies at bay. Is Strine mad? No; the funniest thing about this hugely funny book is that there is no subtext. It really is about being able to take women's clothes off, enter secretly their privacies, and not be caught; and the hilarity is due in large part to the fact that Baker thought he could get away with such a tale, and then did.

There was a film of the early '60s—porn soft to the point of flaccidity—called *The Immoral Mr. Teas*. Mr. Teas, a fussy, mild, secretly horny guy, acquires a pair of glasses that allows him to see through people's clothes. The film had 3D sequences inserted, and the audience was given glasses; every time Mr. Teas put on his glasses, we put on ours, with a somewhat shaming sense of complicity, to see what he saw. What Baker has done is to write in such a way as to make us see what Strine sees, and share his elation and his—it's what he calls it—love.

Late in the book, repletion sets in, and the sense that Baker has bitten off less than he can chew, and the wish for some kind of transcendence, or something different anyway. We get instead a happy, even a fatuously happy ending—which is all right but not the same thing. Maybe there is something limiting about the pornographic eye—"th'expense of spirit in a waste of shame." What's astonishing is that Baker has kept those thoughts from the reader's mind for so long.

1994

The Everlasting Story of Nory
by Nicholson Baker

THERE ARE VERY MANY novelists who have among their works a tour de force—a startling or unlikely achievement, or a brilliant triumph against self-imposed odds, or an immodest display of skill for its own sake. Nicholson Baker is a writer of tours de force who has yet to write a novel. Perhaps that's too stringent or exclusive a judgment, considering the present baffling and baffled state of ambitious novel-writing, but certainly every definition of the tour de force fits *Vox* (book-length phone sex) or *Mezzanine* (endless office trivialities) or *The Fermata* (goofy porno fantasy) and his others, not because of their subjects or modes but because of the exhilarating success they achieve.

His new book is one more. *The Everlasting Story of Nory* is a few months in the life of Eleanor, or Nory, who would be in the fourth grade if she were in America but who is spending a year with her parents and baby brother in England, and going to a blazer-and-rep-tie cathedral school. The book is written in the third person, but the language and the ethos are pervasively those of a smart (but not prodigious) strong (but not fearless) and imaginative (but not poetic) girl of ten, who has many interests and is apprehensive about bad dreams:

> Nory especially disliked when she had teeth dreams. Say, for example, a beautiful graceful fluffer-necked duck that was just sitting away the time in the reeds by a river, its feathers being fluttered by the wind, and when you came up to it in the dream to hold out your hand to it to say hello and give it a piece of bread it would suddenly curl back its beaks and show huge fangy teeth.

Nory's language is a mass of wonderful malapropisms, often ones that suggest a mistaken but not so unlikely shadow meanings that the phrases will probably retain throughout Nory's everlasting life: *a crude awakening, kitten caboodle, bump on a rug, par none, totally made up from scrap.* But it's not just the language that Baker reproduces—or recreates—but the coarse weave of childhood thought, the leaps of memory, apprehension, and association. Only lengthy quotation would do it justice.

Baker does have competition in this sort of ventriloquism, though I would rank his attempt with the best I know of, for instance *Eloise* by Kay Thompson, certain of the Ramona books by Beverley Cleary, and *The Young Visiters* by Daisy Ashford, who however actually was a nine-year-old girl. Like that book, and unlike Cleary's and *Eloise*, Baker's book, though it can be read easily and with pleasure by children, is for grownups. Ten-year-olds may find nothing particularly brilliant in its capturing of minute nuances of their own vagaries of speech and thought; many would probably rate their own literary work as highly as Nory's, and many would be right, which is of course the point; and they might object (my own daughters did) at how much is said and how little is done. In fact grownup readers might too, though I didn't.

Partly for amusement, because she has no close friend in England, partly to lessen the likelihood of bad dreams at night or to stop thinking about them, Nory thinks of stories; she is constantly at work on several, some written (her spelling is wonderfully captured, as idiosyncratic yet universal as her thought-processes) and some told to her dolls or to her brother. There is the life story of Cooch her raccoon doll, the story of the Icy Freezie Day in Autumn, and the amazing Everlasting Life of Mariana. Often her writing ends with her favorite phrase, every writer's pious promise—TO BE CONTINUED.

Nory has firm ideas about what makes for a successful story: You really need something to fail in a story, she thinks, because when it fails it has to get better. How does Baker meet this criterion? His story is mostly less like a Nory story and more like life: more school, more sleeping and getting up, more aimless thought, and fewer gratifying discoveries, coincidences and reversals. Nory considers that the thing that has failed in her own life is that she has no best friend in England, and prospects there are rather poor; she cultivates competitive Kira, but she also befriends (without particularly

The Everlasting Story of Nory *by Nicholson Baker*

liking) the despised and bullied Pamela, and Kira finds this shocking—Nory will ruin her own standing that way. Pamela refuses to complain to her teachers about the bullies, and forbids Nory to as well; she is also pretty unforthcoming and not very pleased with Nory as a friend. Oh well. In the end the Kira/Pamela difficulty works out, maybe a little better, or a little quicker, than it ought to, which is to say more like a story than like life, which the book up to then has not been.

 The language is wonderful, Nory is a wonder too, but it is the secret life led in Nory's stories that are the heart of this book. They are about love and loss and discovery and suffering, about living through the burning rain and recognizing the princess with the yellow hair, about creating your own endings and your own continuings; they are as profound—drawn up from the deeps—as the real ones real children tell, before most of them forget how. It would be unsurprising—though sort of really badly unfair—if Baker has actually transcribed the writings of an actual child (his own daughter?) and put them out under his (and Nory's) name. Because of course now there would be no way to give them back.

1998

The Book of Evidence
by John Banville

"It is September," writes imprisoned murderer Freddie Montgomery in John Banville's new novel *The Book of Evidence*. "I have been here now for two months. It seems longer than that. The tree that I can glimpse from the window of my cell has a drab, dusty look, it will soon begin to turn. It trembles, as if in anticipation; at night I fancy I can hear it, rustling excitedly out there in the dark." The writer of these delicately comic sentiments has committed an atrocious and inexplicable act of violence. As Humbert Humbert opined in similar circumstances, you can count on a murderer for a fancy prose style.

John Banville is an Irish writer less well known in America than in the British Isles, but about to become much better known here (I would venture) on the strength of this singularly accomplished and gripping novel, the "book of evidence" which Freddie Montgomery, expatriate ex-mathematician and wastrel, is compiling while awaiting trial. He wants not to exculpate himself in it, or avoid punishment for his deed, or even to apologize; he seems to want nothing but to stand before the reader, eventually before the court, exactly and fully revealed.

For the chain of circumstances which leads up to, or at least issues in, murder, we have, however, only Freddie's witness; for the truth of his story we have only the evidence of his mordantly comic perceptions. It seems that Freddie, knocking around the Mediterranean with his wife and young son, fell in with an American loafer and drug dealer, from whom he borrowed money without intending to repay it. The don of the island and backer of the American decides to hold Freddie's wife and son as hostages while Freddie goes home and gets money to repay his debt.

But there is no money at Coolgrange, the decayed country seat of his family, where his mother is trying to stay afloat by raising thor-

The Book of Evidence *by John Banville*

oughbred ponies. The only valuable things in the house, the paintings, have been sold cheap to finance this enterprise, ending up, Freddie suspects, in the much grander house of Helmut Behrens, a Berenson-like collector and dealer, with whose imperious daughter Freddie once had a brief but searing affair.

That's where Freddie, snubbed by the Behrenses, comes upon the painting by an anonymous master of the Dutch school, which (he never makes it clear) might have been one of his father's: this painting he steals, the theft of which is interrupted by the innocent maid, the maid foolishly taken hostage, who tried to resist Freddie in his madness. The murder, rendered with nearly unbearable exactness, falls midway in the book; through the rest, Freddie awaits in fear and delicious anticipation his inevitable but strangely delayed arrest.

The Book of Evidence is compared by the publisher to Camus's *The Stranger*, which is quite wrong. The existentialism of *The Stranger*, insofar as it is expressible, implies the taking of responsibility for ourselves and our actions despite their absurd contingency, despite the fact that we find no reason in ourselves to do these actions and not others. Freddie Montgomery's malaise is the much more common fake existentialism indulged in by those who want to take refuge from responsibility in lack of meaning, who find in it a justification for their fecklessness and contempt for humankind, including those who ought to command their love. At the end of his book, Freddie believes himself to be improving, believes he can glimpse a new, chastened person being born out of the old bad Freddie, but the reader may doubt it.

Far more than Camus, the writer we must compare John Banville to in this book is Vladimir Nabokov. The comparison can be quite extensive, in fact, and could include both superficial resemblances of plot and structures and matters of style and substance. Freddie Montgomery is, like Humbert Humbert, sitting in prison following his arrest, writing his explanatory or at least circumstantial account in the form of an address to the judge and jury, who will in fact never hear the evidence. The laceratingly funny pitch-black comedy of Freddie's contemptuous, contemptible self and its adventures in the world of sense-perception reminds us of Nabokov's terrible comedies of murder, of *Despair* and *Laughter in the Dark*.

But above these resemblances, there is the central achievement of *The Book of Evidence*, which also recalls the heart-stopping acrobatics of *Lolita* and *Pale Fire*: a wicked, mad, or at least self-deceived narrator, who in life would fill us with loathing or with clinical indifference; a coruscating brilliance of language in which the narrator's self-perceptions and self-delusions are caught and projected; and the author's continual effort to have the language itself redeem the sinner, make him worthy of a forgiveness he does not otherwise deserve—an effort renewed sentence by sentence, page by page, and more often successful than ought to be possible, shockingly, exhilaratingly successful, so that the reader laughs helplessly aloud in amazement and dismay.

To bring his story to an end, Banville seems to resort to casting an unnecessary and unconvincing Nabokovian shadow of madness and was-it-a-dream uncertainty over his tale at the last moment, as though reaching the shore of the last page were enough, and he had only this last gasp in him. No matter. Only lengthy quotation would suggest the extent to which John Banville has triumphed up until that moment in his enterprise, and better than lengthy quotation would be a copy of the book itself.

1990

≈ ATHENA BY JOHN BANVILLE ≈

*J*OHN BANVILLE'S NEW novel is—though the publisher nowhere admits it, in the book itself or the pre-publication advertising—is the third (perhaps final) volume of a serial novel, which began with *The Book f Evidence* (1989) and continued with *Ghosts* (1993). It may be that the publisher fears that readers who have not read the earlier volumes will not buy this one if they know. Better, apparently, that they should find themselves immersed in something that seems teasingly incomplete. Some American reviewers of *Ghosts* who read it without reference to the first novel—reviewers of novels being under no obligation to research the earlier works of their assigned subjects—were understandably puzzled. For it is indeed part of a series, as ambitious and original a series as Durrell's Alexandria Quartet, and better written. Readers should begin at the beginning.

In the first novel, an atrocious murder is committed in the course of the theft of a priceless painting. All the terms of this original circumstance, like poison pellets, proceed through the tissues of the subsequent novels: murder, painting, theft, atrocious, priceless. Freddie Montgomery, indolent egoist, murderer in *The Book of Evidence*, haunted ex-con and novice art-expert in *Ghosts*, is entangled in *Athena* with a set of 17th century Dutch paintings, apparently the ones recently looted from "Whitewater," country house of art collector Helmut Behrens, the same grand mansion from which Freddie once stole that first painting, in the course of committing the first murder.

He has changed his name now, to Morrow—"I chose it for its faintly hopeful hint of futurity"—and come to a empty house in an out-of-the-way Dublin neighborhood ("The house was in... What shall I call it? Rue Street, that sounds right") to work for the bizarre gang of thieves who have looted Whitewater, cataloguing and authenticating their pictures. He is held there in the otherwise vacant house by a woman, a woman to whom this book is addressed, to whom the events are narrated in which she took part, and who has fled:

"Were you waiting all along to go, poised to leap? It seems to me now that even as I held you clasped in my appalled embrace you were already looking back at me, like one lingering on the brink of departure, all that you were leaving already fading in your glance, becoming memory even as it stood before you. Were you part of the plot, a party to it? I would like to know. I think I would like to know."

The affair with this woman, whom he chooses to address simply as A., is the matter of this book: the steadily escalating intensity of it, the minute physical actualities of it, above all the continuous permeation of the surroundings by it—air, weather, skyscapes. He learns next to nothing of her, and what little he is told he doesn't know whether to believe or not. It is she who raises the stakes, again and again, linking sex to pain and abasement and the telling of dreadful secrets, finally getting from him his awful story. It only increases her heat.

As dangerous, hilarious, exalting, entangling as the affair is the language in which it is cast: they are not different. This should not need to be said except that it is so rarely achieved to this degree: Nabokov in *Lolita* and *Laughter in the Dark* come to mind: "Her miniature feet were of a reddish hue, and curiously splayed at the toes, betokening a barefoot childhood spent in some gaudy, aquatic region of mud and magnolia and shrieking birds. Oh, my Manon, where are you?"

The sharply delimited world of *Athena* (the intense affair, the single street, a small cast of comic supporting characters) drifts like a lifeboat on the dark waters of the earlier books. We who have read them know that this man has a wife in his past, and a child, whom he once left as hostages to a drug-lord in Mallorca; that he once also had an affair of comparable intensity with the heiress of Whitewater. And there is the Professor who may have once falsely certified a famous painting owned by Behrens; and there is the murdered chambermaid. And through the city of *Athena* women are being murdered, atrociously, by a serial killer.

And yet dense and involved as this net of plot is, it is in a sense

Athena by John Banville

irrelevant, and never completed, perhaps not able to be completed. It is like the mythological subjects of the paintings the narrator studies, the occasion for the achieving of certain effects, and otherwise unimportant. Freddie has always been an unreliable narrator, a connoisseur of his own sensations whether pleasing or harrowing, to whom the world otherwise remains opaque or illusory. But the reader now and then suspects that he is not only misrepresenting but creating, that on certain pages his author draws close enough to him to grant him a share in the inventing of the story he is supposed to be only living.

"I felt myself carried off to other times and other, imaginary places: a spring day in Clichy (I have never been in Clichy), a hot, thundery evening on a road somewhere in North Africa (never been there either), a great, high, panelled room in an ancient chateau with straw-coloured sunlight on the faded tapestries and someone practicing on a spinet (though I have never seen a spinet or heard one played). Where do they come from, these mysterious, exalted flashes that are not memories yet seem far more than mere imaginings?"

They come, of course, from his author, provider of those and of every spasm and every crime. More than of the (imaginary) Flemish and Dutch artists he so lovingly and wittily brings to life, Banville's work reminds me of Tiepolo—the transparency, the presence of the artist's gesture everywhere, the frank brushwork admitting that what is to be enjoyed here is not only what is created but the artist's delight in creating. In place of Tiepolo's blue aerial spaces and sun-washed cleanliness we have squalor, betrayal, obsession, cigarette ends. The difference is less material than it seems. John Banville is a splendid and daring writer at the height of his powers, and his central theme is his own moving hand and eye: his theme is Delight.

1996

SOME NONFICTIONS

The Mask of Nostradamus
～ by James Randi ～

*M*ost people accept the possibility of prophecy, just as they believe (without thinking about it in any analytic way) in the efficaciousness of wishes passionately held, in poetic justice, in precognition and psychic insight. We live most of our lives in an unconsidered prerationality, and find no difficulty with it. Difficulties only arise when a systematic mind takes up such beliefs, and meets another systematic mind bent on dismantling them.

Michel de Nostredame was an astrologer and almanac-maker of the sixteenth century, who used a Latinized form of his name, as scholars of his time often did: Nostradamus. In addition to the usual predictions accompanying his almanacs, Nostradamus compiled a lengthy series of quatrains, crabbed and obscure—automatic writing almost—which were claimed to be prophetic of events that would take place years, even centuries on. For reasons that even James Randi fails to make clear to me, this collection of prophecies and not other similar ones generated in that century or earlier centuries has persisted, has gained rather than lost authority, and is proverbial now as a Book of Knowledge in which the wise can descry the shape of the future.

The squaring off of Nostradamus and his believers with James Randi is a wonderful idea. Randi is of course "The Amazing Randi," skilled stage magician and master of illusion, who like Houdini before him has devoted a large part of his career to unmasking those who use the techniques of stage magic to pretend to supranormal powers. He was the nemesis of Uri Geller (Randi could bend spoons too, and told how Geller did it) and recipient for his educational efforts of a MacArthur Foundation "genius grant," the choice of Randi being a bit of genius in itself.

How does he match up against the old mage? It ought to be said that Randi's opponents are really the later interpreters and not

Nostradamus himself, toward whom he takes a patronizing but not ferocious attitude: this distinction may account for the otherwise obscure title of his book. It ought also to be said that Randi is not really a scholar of sixteenth-century intellectual trends, or anywhere near as able at manipulating historical tools and materials as he is in manipulating scarves, swords and rabbits.

"Though we may look to the Renaissance for poetry and music," he writes, setting the background for Nostradamus, "not much really brave, hard thought took place." Now it is possible to suppose that the thought of Calvin, Machiavelli, Erasmus, and Paolo Sarpi concerned itself with matters no longer considered central—with God, or with how a Christian society should work, how princes should behave, what constitutes justice—but that certainly does not make it less brave or less hard. Randi seems to believe that at any age and at any time, the wheat is easily separated from the chaff, the hard bright truths from the stuff and nonsense, and is unforgiving of past thinkers who mixed the two: they ought somehow to have known better.

In addition to his wooden lack of sympathy with past intellectual endeavor, Randi is given to odd unscholarly procedures (he cites an 1848 edition of the *Encyclopedia Britrannica* as an authority, for instance). He has assembled rather than constructed his book, in a random cut-and-paste fashion that strikes a reader as rather medieval, though I suspect the word processor is in fact responsible; he makes room in it for multiple diversions and digressions, a disquisition on Hermes Trismegistus, a life of the English astrologer John Dee that is full of small errors.

None of this would matter much if it didn't occupy so much of a short book. For when Randi settles down to demolishing the Nastradamians, he comes brilliantly into his own. Nostradamus is supposed by his latter-day flacks to have predicted the French Revolution, Napoleon, and Hitler's rise, among other things, and Randi takes up several of the key quatrains on which believers have relied. He not only makes effective fun of their hopelessly inadequate methods of analysis, but makes some striking analyses of his own of what Nostradamus might have actually been thinking about. Here Randi genuinely engages with the past to solve the mysteries of a difficult text, rooting the quatrains convincingly in the geography of Michel de Nostredame's youth and the events of his day.

The Mask of Nostradamus *by James Randi*

There should have been more of this kind of work in the book. I suspect that the reason there is not is that Nostradamus actually turns out to be quick work to demolish. The constructions of his later promoters vanish into (hot) air as soon as they are looked at closely. Like the tonic bottles of the medicine showman, the prophecies of Nostradamus are but the center of a rhetorical invention, and uninteresting in themselves.

Well, we might have known. But then again—though Randi and his fellow hardheads gnash their teeth—the unmasking of one or a dozen instances of false prophecy will not keep most of us from pondering others, or noting occult urgings or prophetic dreams, usually to forget them again when they yield no result. The committed battlers over prophecy and the occult—those who believe such things are Really Really True and those who can prove they're Really Really Not True—are the minority, locking horns while the rest of us watch bemused.

1996

The Queen's Conjuror
By Benjamin Woolley

*R*ATHER THAN GROWING smaller with distance, the past seems continually to enlarge as we go forward: the farther away we get the more we learn. Think of how our conception of magic in western intellectual history has changed: Forty years ago D.P. Walker made his ground-breaking typology of magic and magical practice in the Renaissance, resurrecting a world-view which though it was wholly unlike our own was internally consistent and astonishingly rich. Frances Yates showed how the magician's high valuation of human intellectual power and passion for method made the growth of what we call science possible. Her studies of magical mnemonics also made clear, though, how very unlike ours these minds of the Renaissance were.

In this tradition stands Benjamin Woolley's new biography of John Dee, Elizabethan scientist and magus (there is really no single term that describes a man like Dee accurately). Dee was born in 1527 and lived till 1609, a long life for the times, and for centuries after his death was regarded either as a figure of fun, a white-bearded would-be sorcerer and dupe; or as the possessor of mystic secrets, maker of gold, seer. Frances Yates first demonstrated that Dee was in fact a major Renaissance figure, who promoted Copernican astronomy, navigation and exploration, and a mathematical understanding of natural law.

There's no getting around the fact, though, that by Dee's own reckoning his greatest enterprise was the lengthy conversations he held for many years with some very unlikely angels, the language of Adam that they taught him, and the universal reformation of the world they promised he would be spearheading.

John Dee is unusual not only in his story but in how much we can know about him: few Elizabethans left as many intimate records. Not only did he keep extensive diaries—of his activities, his dreams, diseases, copulations with his wife, children's troubles—but he recorded all the conversations he held with those angels, who came to his houses in England and Europe and spoke (usually) out of a crystal ball.

Actually, Dee never spoke directly to or heard the voice of an angel. The angels spoke through a medium, Edward Kelley, a man much younger than Dee and an even stranger soul. Kelley arrived at Dee's house in Mortlake, up the Thames from London, in March of 1582, and that first night saw figures in the "showstone" that Dee put before him. Before he ceased "skrying" five years later in Prague (whence the angels had led the two of them and their families) he had transmitted hundreds of pages of their hectoring, teasing, teaching, warning and play-acting, as well as an unimaginably tedious method of taking down and totting up a universal language said to be that of men before the Flood.

After the first weeks, Dee never doubted that Edward Kelley was receiving messages from spirits. Nor did anyone else who heard about the work the two were doing. The doubt everyone had was what *kind* of spirits they were: good or bad? Angelic or demonic? Fallen or unfallen? If bad, then John Dee and Kelley were endangering their immortal souls; if good, though, what knowledge might they not transmit? It certainly wasn't a simple question. These angels—standard ones like Michael and Uriel at first, then others like Il, dressed all in red, and Galvage, an old woman, and little Madimi, a sprite who grows into a fearsome challenging temptress—contradict themselves, curse the enemies of God, snap at Dee and Kelley, laugh and chat and pray. They resemble the spirit guides of the modern medium, and are no doubt the same thing, whatever thing that exactly is; few mediums though are capable of producing, apparently entirely ad lib, the truly moving or startling passages of prophecy and adjuration that Kelley could.

The conversations lasted till the two men and their appalled but apparently obedient wives fulfilled the angel Madimi's final commandment: that they have their spouses in common. Dee himself was astonished that God's angel could command such a thing, but he did it, or at least attempted it. The record is clear, and a unique record it is: four Elizabethans, Dee, Kelley, Dee's somewhat fiery wife Jane, and Kelley's wife Joanna, in the Prague of magic and alchemy, obeying naked Madimi ("she sheweth her shame also," Dee notes) and bedding down together—in the same room, Woolley has determined.

Odder still, the angelic communications end there, and are never taken up again: whether by Kelley's choice or Dee's, whether out of fear or confusion or shame, is unknown. Dee returned to England and disappointment, never gaining the influence or position he knew he was fitted for. Kelley remained in Prague and after a raffish career as an alchemist, vanishes. He is a popular Prague legend today, along with Faust and the Golem.

Woolley's biography of Dee is a model of popular history in many ways. He is not always comfortable in the thought-world of Dee, and has little to add to the understanding of spiritual magic, but his management of sources is exemplary; he finds illuminating connections everywhere, has hunted down (almost) every character Dee ever encountered, and arranged a rackety and confusing career intelligibly (he might have spent more pages on Dee's later life). As someone who has been involved imaginatively with Dee's and Kelley's adventures for twenty years, I am amazed to see it all pulled together so masterfully. Whether uniquely strange, or only strange because of how much we happen to know of them, these minds of the past step forward in this book undeniably, obstreperously real.

2001

Fragments for a History of the Human Body: Parts I, II, III, edited by Michel Feher

*H*ERE ARE THREE LARGE volumes, each over 400 pages long, collectively titled *Fragments for a History of the Human Body*, attractively produced and purporting to be numbers of a journal called *Zone*, though they have few or none of the features of the average journal. Drawn to the irresistible topic, a casual or "lay" reader opens the first volume and looks into a dense and almost secretive introduction by the editor, Michel Feher: no hints on how the volumes came to be, or whether the articles were specially commissioned, or what in general is up here.

"The history of the human body is not so much the history of its representations as of its modes of construction," says the editor, suggesting that bodies do not exist except as they are defined by those who have them: the body is constructed by the imagination. Such a history can "turn the body into a thoroughly historicized and completely problematic issue." The lay reader soon senses himself to be in dense academic woods, amid new and perhaps conflicting methodologies, and far from the friendly purviews of a Lewis Thomas or a Stephen Jay Gould.

Never mind. He dips into a piece in the middle volume by Hillel Schwartz, "The Three-Body Problem and the End of the World," a divagation on Cyril Connolly's remark that inside every fat man there is a thin man signaling wildly to get out. Schwartz draws on a vast range of reference to describe the various bodies we feel inside ourselves: pre-Freudian psychotheraphy, the history of kleptomania and anorexia, hunger artists (including Cavanagh, "the Irish impostor") and *délire des négations*, or the conviction that one does not in fact have a body at all.

This extraordinary piece suggests a danger in a history of "modes of construction" as opposed to mere "representations": the danger of sliding too easily from the analysis of metaphor to its deployment in the service of understanding, a slippery path for argument to take. Schwartz's three bodies—the sweet thin body of youth, the streamlined transformed body of the future, the fat body of the present—move a bit suddenly from clever conceit to simple fact: "Slimming has become the primary Western solution to the Three-Body Problem." Other essays attempt the same trick without Schwartz's brilliance and dissolve in (hot) air.

The lay reader learns quickly to skip the unrewarding essays, for there are riches all around, and stories strange but true, and things he will not have heard before. Thomas Laqeur takes up the discovery of the clitoris in the 16th century by Columbus (Renaldus Columbus, no relation) and ponders what it means to "discover" an organ well known to antiquity. A case can be made for Columbus, just as a case can be made for Freud's "discovery" that as a woman matures the locus of orgasm moves from clitoris to vagina: the "discovery" is of a new construction of female sexuality and how it functions—or ought to function, in the mind of the discoverer. Freud, according to Laqeur, knew as well as any 19th-century physiologist that the vagina has few neural connections and that the clitoris is rich in them; but he believed that a woman could—and should—transfer her sexuality to the more socially responsible spot, in preparation for heterosexual intercourse.

This and another essay by Laqeur—on why prostitutes have historically been considered barren—can be set beside a piece by Caroline Walker Bynum on the female body and religious experience in the Middle Ages. She like Laqeur can show that male and female only recently came to be regarded as opposites; until after the Renaissance, the relation was more commonly perceived as inside/outside, or higher/lower: the female was the lesser being inside the larger male being, though the male (even the male God of Christianity) grew inside the female; the male sex organs were the female sex organs turned inside out.

Bynum's and Laquer's essays strike the reader as models of what work in history should do—disabuse us moderns of our illusion of complete originality, and mitigate the imbalance of a simple "evolutionary" or progressive view of history. Bynum disposes of the assumption that Christianity has been anti-physical or misogynistic in any simple way; medieval female religious experience was often intensely somatic, and the central Christian concept of an incarnate God had strange implications for his carnate children.

If the notion that the body is actually constructed by and not merely represented in the imagination seems too extreme a formulation, consider Bynum's evidence about the physical religious experiences of women in the middle ages—stigmata, miraculous inedia (not eating but thriving anyway), catatonic trances, ecstatic nosebleeds, mystical lactations and pregnancies. Such phenomena, she says, appear generally for the first time in the 12th and 13th centuries, which to her suggests that the body, in particular the female body, may actually have a history.

Impossible to digest (digestion is a big topic here), these volumes are also hard to put away. How much of the contents can a brief notice describe? The introduction suggests a rough plan to the three volumes, but the lay reader would no more want to follow such a scheme than to eat his way through a long menu from beginning to end.

So may we suggest beginning with the Bynum and Laquer; refreshing the palate with an amazing suite of color photographs showing what the Wodaabe nomads of Niger think gorgeous men look like; then hitting "The Art of Pulling Teeth in the Sixteenth and Seventeenth Centuries" (the rotten tooth a symbol of vice). Taste Mark Elvin's long essay on a totally different construction of the body (the Chinese) and its 20th-century transformations. Alternatively, try William R. LaFleur's analysis of the hungry ghosts of Japanese Buddhism, and how a moral allegory can be "somaticized" and turned into a physical explanation—in this case, an explanation for what becomes of feces dropped by the wayside. The text by J.C. Beaune on "The Classical Age of Automata" is so highly articulated that it falls into pieces, like a puppet; lots of Strange But True facts, though, and the pictures are fun. For dessert, don't miss Piero Camporesi on the round of sacred bread whose implications were enthusiastically elaborated by Baroque Jesuit writers: How long does the Eucharist actually remain the flesh of God in the dissolving bowels? For about 20 minutes, the Fathers thought.

1989

Wonders and the Order of Nature 1150–1750 by Lorraine Daston and Katherine Park

"*It's not that I'm curious,*" my great-aunt Anne used to say, "I just want to know." She was expressing an age-old disapproval of curiosity that has roots in the Church Fathers, particularly Augustine. Curiosity was a form of lust, a wandering cupidity of the eye and the mind as potentially sinful as that of the body. Not only are we not to be curious about our neighbors' business and things that don't concern us; we should avoid peering uselessly and impertinently into God's creation as well. The appropriate emotion when contemplating creation was wonder, which marvels but does not seek to pry. How these two complementary impulses, curiosity and wonder, changed (and sometimes swapped) meanings, moral worth, objects and consequences over the course of eight or 10 centuries is the hugely ambitious subject of this large, handsome and endlessly intriguing book.

Wonders have a history, and different sorts of things have counted as wonders at different times. What counts as the order of nature changes, and what sticks out from, tests, transcends or violates that order has to change as well. Medieval writers generally considered that marvels were frequent in faraway places but rare in the center of the world (that is, the Mediterranean countries). Somewhere in Africa or Asia or the Antipodes were races of people with dog's heads, or whose heads grew below their shoulders, or trees that bore gourds inside which were perfect little lambs; somewhere there were petrifying springs or unicorns or one-legged Sciopodes or all the marvels that Othello brags to Desdemona he has seen. In far-off Ireland, there were geese that grew from barnacles (monks were allowed to eat them on Fridays, as not really being meat). For all the medieval writer knew, anything was possible out there, and there was no philosophical principle that could hinder God's creativity.

But there were other kinds of wonders, and other forms of wonder, that were more problematic. If lots of far-off wonders showed God's creative powers, individual wonders close at hand might portend God's anger. Conjoined twins, two-headed cows, meteors and double suns were "monsters" or "portents" or "prodigies," all words indicating that something was being shown or predicted or brought about, usually something very bad. (Among the many fascinating illustrations in the book are a couple of anatomically correct medieval relics of famous conjoined twins, set among the gargoyles and demons decorating medieval institutions.) The question about stories of wonders and monsters of this kind was not so much Is it true? as What does it mean?

It was the study of some medieval writers to make wonders cease. Albertus and Aquinas wanted attention paid to universals and not particulars; wonder was akin to fear and shock and arose from ignorance of general principles and causes. The contrast between those who know and those who don't is constant from Albertus down to the present, even as the valuation of wonder and curiosity changes: Sometimes the elite and the educated can appreciate wonders that common people are too coarse to marvel at—wonders of art, rare gems, automata, coral, sea shells—and sometimes the ignorant and the vulgar marvel at things that the philosopher knows to be part of the order of nature and therefore not wonders at all.

Few philosophers of nature—from the Schoolmen through the Renaissance thinkers whom the authors cleverly describe as "preternaturalists" (those who saw occult forces, astral powers, demonic intelligences and the power of the imagination as generators of wonders) down to sobersides Bacon and Descartes—failed to test their theories of knowledge on the subject of wonders, artificial and natural, foreign or domestic. Is Nature an artist, tossing off "sports" for the sheer creative delight of it, or is Nature itself art—inert matter shaped by God in wholly rational ways according to His plan? Robert Boyle thought that even thinking of "Nature" as an active force took away from the glory due to God alone.

As jampacked with stuff as the great collections of the Renaissance princes which are among its continuing subjects, *Wonders and the Order of Nature* defies summary; reading it and trying to keep in mind the constantly and subtly shifting meanings of a dozen or so key terms is dizzying but fun. The same themes and problems, even the same wonders and the same remarks about them, return again and again in a sort of tidal fashion that can be lulling as well as delightful, and curiosity is indulged and sated over and over. But at length a vital historical argument comes clear.

It is a common assumption that the taming of wonders and the ceasing of miracles proceed steadily as human kind "grows up," that portents and prodigies and the thrill of the uncanny are given up along with witchcraft trials and sun-centered astronomy as science "matures." The authors show that wonders never ceased, that the rationalist savants of the Age of Enlightenment never even began a thorough program of explaining away the accumulated wonders of the centuries, and that the very idea of a human "childhood" transcended by the growth of science is itself an Enlightenment myth. In fact, the intellectual establishment of Europe in the 18th century was reacting to a century of turmoil and terror, in which wonders—portents, prodigies and monsters—were used in the overthrowing of prelates and princes, Catholic and Protestant. To argue that the age of miracles was over, that the greatest wonder of Nature was its instant and steady production of commonplace effects and tidy replications, that the job of the wise was to employ a suitable curiosity in discovering the mechanisms of this regularity—this was a political and social program as much as a philosophical one. The skeptical smile of the 18th-century savant suggests that he at last has outgrown childish things.

But skeptics have been as common as enthusiasts in any age. The Emperor Frederick II in the 13th century sent to Ireland for barnacle-covered driftwood, and wrote that "none... of these shellfish exhibit[ed] any form of a bird." He decided he didn't believe the story; probably it arose, he thought, because no one knew where the geese actually nested. Robert Moray, however, in the enlightened 17th century, thought he saw tiny birds growing in the shells. Voltaire believed in "maternal impression": pregnant women scared by bloodshed could have children with bloodstain birthmarks. My great-aunt Anne thought so too.

An entire further volume, in fact, could have been written about the persistence of wonders in 19th-century America: the discovery of "deep time" and its wonders (dinosaurs, mammoths); the building of dime museums like Barnum's, popular versions of the aristocratic *Wunderkammern* of Renaissance Europe; and the history of "freaks" displayed for the sake of entertainment, exotic thrills and uncanny fear. The cover picture on this book is a painting of a girl, beautiful in a Renaissance gown, who has exactly the genetic hirsuteness that "Jo Jo the Dog-faced Boy" exhibited to crowds in this century, and that Lon Chaney Jr. modeled his makeup on in *The Wolfman*. Maybe the contrary valuations of wonder, curiosity, amazement and the marvelous are not actually historical at all but cognitive programs with a certain maximum of alternative outcomes—programs running on that marvel of marvels, the human brain.

1998

COMIX

~ BEN KATCHOR ~

A SINGULAR FEATURE OF cultural life in the twentieth century is the way in which so many popular genres and modes of entertainment have been adopted by artists with ambitions different from, even opposite to, those of the creators and marketers who made the forms popular. This is somewhat different from the occurrence within the popular genres themselves of great and powerful creators (a D.W. Griffith in movies, a Raymond Chandler in crime fiction) who are committed to the original impulses of their genre or medium and merely infuse it with their particular genius. I'm speaking of the special elation we feel when a creator, though very likely drawn to a medium or mode in the first place because of the power it has shown in its popular manifestations, applies a different kind of intelligence, a new eye and sensibility, to it: when Francois Truffaut produces *The 400 Blows*, or Bob Dylan releases *Blonde on Blonde*. When, in other words, the archetypal force, the limited moral palette, the easily graspable oppositions and a-gun-and-a-girl stories of popular culture are transmuted or are abandoned altogether, and ambiguity, acute consciousness, allusion and private insight come in.

The comic strip is one of those popular genres, and it has had its geniuses: Winsor McKay (*Little Nemo in Slumberland*) and George Herriman (*Krazy Kat*) are two, and I would class Walt Kelly (*Pogo*) with them, though his was an art more mixed—aesthetically and in ambition—than theirs. Like D.W. Griffith and Chaplin, they arose within their medium, advancing its possibilities by their power but in general serving its original purposes. In the late 1960s—when almost every day you awoke to find some startling takeover or transformation had occurred in some realm of popular culture (the Beach Boys are reinventing surfing music! Science fiction is modernist literature!)—the comic strip too was seized upon, and in the underground papers Victor Moscoso, Kim Deitch and Robert Crumb were raiding its history for lines (both words and pen-strokes) and motifs to make wholly personal art with.

Now, of course, film and popular music and the comic strip are available for any and all uses, classic, parodic, self-referential or wholly original and with hardly a nod to the language and gesture of the historical medium—the same evolution or devolution that earlier happened to the novel. This fact should make the appearance of a weird new comic strip at the bottom of the page in our favorite low-circulation independent paper, a strip actually not comic and indeed without any observable designs on us, no particular puzzlement. There are lots of them, and I know people who regard Ben Katchor's *Julius Knipl: Real Estate Photographer* as just another one. I do not. I am as surprised and moved by its existence as if it had effected an alchemical transmutation of its medium all by itself.

The eponymous Julius Knipl, about whom we learn very little, is really not a character at all but an observer, curious, maybe even a voyeur in a small way. The subject of the strip is his city: a sort of shabby hypnogogic New York that, like Terry Gilliam's *Brazil*, takes place "somewhere in the 20th Century." It is the very city where I find myself in dreams so often and for no reason (not my childhood landscape, not the place my life ever took place). Katchor's city differs from mine in many respects, but in one way distinctly: here everything can be read, not only the names of stores and restaurants and businesses (Regularity Cafeteria, the Lacoon Hotel, Mansoyl Towel and Apron Supply, Euxine School of Dance) but the names of products (Mother of Mercy aspirin, Gobang Cosmetics, Next O'Kin brand sardines) and even the styles on boxes of false eyebrows (the Olivier, the Guinness, the Skulnick). The hilarious strange familiarity of these names, and there are some in nearly every strip, are one element of the Katchor effect, along with the cast of sadsack small businessmen and obsessives with odd spiritual longings, the dark wash that turns day night and night melancholy, and the Borgesian or even Kafkaesque secret histories described in the top or narrative bar of the strip (does this feature have a name? I don't know it). To retail one of these histories as continuous prose communicates something, but maybe the wrong thing:

"A siren in the middle of the night arouses vague unease and idle curiosity. Fortunately a group of dedicated volunteers gather each night in a rent-free office, equipped with a short-wave radio, to monitor the evening's assorted sirens and alarms. The members of the Siren Query Brigade are a hearty lot who thrive on little sleep and the misfortunes of others. A call comes in, and within moments receives a sure and comforting reply. The anonymous caller expresses his appreciation, and goes back to sleep." Mr. Knipl learns from the Brigade that the siren that woke him was just a "one-alarm fire at the Fricasee Club on Pastoral Avenue." He goes back to sleep: "Nothing to do with me."

Katchor has recently been branching out or pushing on. His recent collection of strips included a long previously unpublished story about the Evening Combinator, the paper that gives news of what people in the city are dreaming ("Mosquito Gives Birth to Sentient Safety Pin.") The compulsive but fitful sleepers, whose dreams are interfering with the waking life of the city, are opposed by Ormond Bell and his devotees at Bell's Stay-Awake-Atorium ("hot coffee, hard chairs"). The beauty and fascination of this tale, as of many of the single strips, is its dreamlike cogency—that sense we have in dreams (Freud identified it) of everything being at once unknown and familiar: the events make momentary sense as they go by, the nonsense allusions do not startle, or wouldn't if we heard them while asleep. Read when awake they are very funny, and their fatuity tugs astonishingly at the heart.

Now Katchor has released a book-length story, *A Jew of New York*. It is what is now being called a "graphic novel," a medium around for a long time in the form of books for children and the semi-literate. It was adopted by the new cartoon artists and their French counterparts (transforming American popular cultural models and then returning them home again being a French specialty) and was brought to mass attention with *Maus*, the Holocaust novels of Art Spiegelman. The ambition of Spiegelman's two volumes astonished readers unfamiliar with the new cartoon art—novelistic breadth communicated by rapid cartoon treatment, at once chillingly distant and immediate, realistic and fable-like.

Katchor's ambitions in *A Jew of New York* are also large, but not so immediately noticeable; his work is also historical, also a gloss on the history of the Jews in America. Set in the 1830s, it seems in the first place to be a surprising departure from the Knipl milieu, but it may also be viewed as a story about the forebears of the mystics, dreamers, entrepreneurs and obsessives of Julius Knipl's city.

It is also—unlike a lot of graphic novels, not to mention contemporary non-graphic ones—a highly finished story, with incident enough for a three-volume novel of its purported period, brilliantly worked out, full of surprises and reverses and all done up at the end. Not unlike the miniature novels of Edward Gorey (surely one of Katchor's forebears) it summons up in a few pages all the machinery and all the accoutrements of a work many times its length. It's odd for a reviewer to hold a book of a mere hundred pages, mostly not covered with text, and realize he will never be able to mention all the things it contains.

The tale has its beginnings in fact. Mordecai Noah, an American Jew of wealth and influence in Jacksonian America, playwright, American Consul in Tunis, and an ardent advocate and defender of the Jewish people, conceived a plan for buying Grand Island in the Niagara River and turning it into an American homeland for the Jews: not only the Jews emigrating from the Old World but the native Jews of the New World, that is the Lost Tribes whom the European settlers called Indians. It was to be an agricultural colony, which would refute the anti-Semitic slander that Jews were unproductive non-cultivators. On September 15, 1825—first day of the Hebrew month of Tishre—Noah, dressed as a "Judge of Israel" in a costume borrowed from the Park Theatre in Buffalo (it was Richard III's, ominously) led a procession of colonists, Indians and well-wishers in a dedication ceremony, though there weren't enough boats on hand to get them all to "Ararat," as the island had been renamed.

Less unusual than it seems—there were of course a thousand Utopian schemes afoot in 1830s America—Noah's idea wasn't even unique: several attempts were made to found a homeland for the Jews in America, including one by Moses E. Levy to bring them all to several hundred acres he owned in Florida, an offer whose time had not yet come. The idea that the native Americans were the Lost Tribes was also not Noah's, but was circulating among a number of thinkers or wonderers, who were assembling evidence from language and custom (Katchor employs this theorizing wonderfully). Noah's schemes and ideas were also typical of many others in failing entirely, unusual only in how fast they failed.

So as Katchor's story begins, most of the people of New York have only dim memories of Ararat; Major Noah and the procession to Grand Island are stories told at the Shearith Batsal Burial Society, and are also to be the subject of the new comedy this season at the New World Theater, titled *The Jew of New York*.

Around the writing, staging, rewriting (by the mysterious and dreadful masked anti-Semite Dr. Solidus) and eventual catastrophic failure of the new comedy are woven other stories, all eventually as in a Dickens novel to knit together. There is the story of the banished Nathan Kishon, formerly the *shoykhet* or ritual butcher of the Shearith Batsal community, fired for an error involving beef tongues, who returns to New York after five years in the wilderness ("On that same August afternoon in the year 1830 a man smelling strongly of animal blood and urine disembarks from the Albany steamboat."). Where has he been? As in any good novel of its period, Kishon tells his long story to another character, Mr. Marah, importer of religious goods and women's hosiery: how he watched Major Noah and his procession to Ararat; how he met there a beaver trapper, a baptized Jew who had lived so long in the woods that he preferred sleeping outdoors ("I was born Moishe Ketzelbourd, but the Indians call me Maurice Cougar") and whose business partner Kishon became.

Ketzelbourd's beaver pelts, and his masturbatory obsession with the now aging theatrical star Miss Patella and her lurid posters (Miss Patella as "Florida" in *The Flume of Youth*); Mr. Marah's new-style "fleshings" or invisible hosiery, certified by the Rabbi of Toulouse as filling "an urgent need in the sphere of public decency," allowing the likes of Miss Patella to appear on stage in *Artemis at Bunker Hill* and other plays apparently naked but actually fully clothed; Kishon's own adoption of the outdoor life, and his inheriting of the Ketzelbourd stock of pelts when Ketzelbourd comes to believe himself a beaver; the appearance of Enoch Letushim, Jew of Palestine, carrying his bag of soil from the Holy Land for the Jews of the New World to mingle with their grave-earth, and his involvement with the man who plans to carbonate Lake Erie and pump the healthful fluid throughout New York—all these stories and many others revolve and meet, merge and part, reflecting and refracting with the apparent endlessness that is characteristic of both Kabbalistic wordplay and the fiction of the heroic age now past. To watch (one does *watch*) a bullock's heart, a mother-of-pearl button, a kippered herring, proceed through the story gaining meaning as it goes, is to watch a supple fictional imagination at work.

The fascination that the Utopian future long held for Americans, indeed for the world, seems to have transmuted, at the millennium's end, into a fascination with understanding or reimagining the past, not only its visions and its hopeless hopes and cruelties and possibilities, but its language as well. Thomas Pynchon's astonishing pastiche in *Mason & Dixon*, telling a late-20th century version of an 18th-century story in his own dream-version of 18th-century prose, is only the most prominent example; Katchor's is another. On the subject of "fleshings" and the Jews, Mr. Kishon the failed butcher holds a conversation with a man in an India-rubber suit: "What sort of attraction do you think lured our co-religionists out of the ghetto and into the mainstream of European culture? Was it the wit of Moliere or the ingenious stage mechanism of Pixérecourt? Or was it simply the opportunity to cast an eye, without shame, upon the living, unclad human form . . . ?"

Everybody in the book talks this way; occasionally a swatch of language will be enclosed in quote marks or even given a shy footnote, but most of it is doubtless Katchor's own, and very oddly has almost no shadow of parody or exaggeration; it feels like the language of books and pamphlets, sub-literary bloviating, and ordinary polite conversation as we know it from fiction. Even the diatribe of Mr. Pettersham of the Anti-Masturbation League has the authentic sound: "For God's sake, even the whoremonger contributes in some small way to the health of the economy. But these sons of Onan have set themselves apart from all palpable reality . . . Cast off your bed rags! Release yourself from the tyranny of the water closet!" ("An entire world of customers is lost to us each day through this wasteful habit," comments a watching businessman.)

Katchor deploys the new proliferation in the 19th century of public writing, posters and shop signs, fliers and menus and packaging—advertising's first age, as Mr. Knipl's milieu is its senescence—to the same end of surreal authenticity, an endless cycling of weird ideas and plans, intersecting as the character's hopes and obsessions do, and providing the Katchor background which threatens to become foreground. Of the dozens of these (the menu of the

American Hotel, with choice of Turtle or Oarlock Soup, Hill of Beef with Andalusian Onion, Galvanic Pickles and Tower of Babel Cake) the most wondrous is the double-spread front end-papers, showing the (proposed) Lake Erie Soda-Water Company system, spreading vascularly throughout the city, with a minute listing of both private and public fountains (there is one at the World Levellers' Society, one at the War Canoe Club, one at the Million Dollar Spirit Church, one at the "Soc. for Hand-washing.") The dull drivel of past ambition and the dark age of hand-set type settle on the spirit with hilarious oppression.

The sadness of *The Jew of New York* is like that of the Knipl strips, though more complex, less evanescent, grounded in a reality (anti-Semitism) that goes unmentioned in Knipl's New York. It is a profound work, weird only to the degree that it is affecting. What has to be said, however, is that Katchor as graphic artist often stumbles along behind Katchor as story-teller and *flaneur*. In short takes, one day at a time, his scratchy drawing and inexpressive faces are part of the amusement, part of the *so nu?* resignation to inefficacy and incompleteness. Over many pages of historical recreation, however, Katchor's inability to express people's insides by graphic gesture is a handicap. George Herriman (*Krazy Kat*) was able in his late reduced and shorthand style still to communicate an inside in this way. Katchor comes out of the current delight in the drawing of people who can't draw (Roz Chast is only the first who comes to mind) and proceeds with a childlike combination of painful thoroughness and slovenliness, so different from his elegant swift prose, a counterweight to it of course and intentional probably, but at book length somewhat wearying. Comic-strip artists are frequently equally accomplished at both aspects of their medium, moving narrative and still picture, though genius is rare in either and banality common; achievements like *The Jew of New York* are therefore to be welcomed, and even hugged to the bosom.

1998

KRAZY KAT: THE COMIC ART OF GEORGE HERRIMAN, BY PATRICK MCDONNELL, KAREN O'CONNELL AND GEORGIA RILEY DE HAVENON

*T*HE UNIQUELY 20TH-Century art of the comic strip requires a unique combination of talents: for drawing, for storytelling and for language. That may be why there have been so few great practitioners among so many strips. I count three, in fact: Winsor McKay ("Little Nemo in Slumberland"), Walt Kelly ("Pogo") and George Herriman, the creator of "Krazy Kat" and the subject of this excellent anthology.

Most people who now remember "Krazy Kat" remember the strip in its last phase—a fluid but essentially unchanging triangle. Krazy Kat loves Ignatz the mouse, who detests Krazy Kat, and continually tosses bricks at the Kat's head to prove it. A cop, Officer Pup, secretly in love with Krazy Kat, pursues and punishes the mouse for his cruelty.

For 20 years, until Herriman's death in 1944, that was its form, a sort of austere and reflective *commedia dell'arte* set in an ever-changing but also static Navajo-flavored Southwest. But in fact, as documented by the authors of this volume, the evolution of "Krazy Kat"—and its creator—to this state was long and varied.

Herriman was born in 1880 in New Orleans, and his origins were—as he might have put it—"shrouded in mystery." He never talked about it, but there is every likelihood that he was of African American descent. His birth certificate classifies him as "colored," though certainly he lived as a white man all his life, and amid the profusion of his early work there is more than one stereotypical black character.

The comic strip was just getting underway when Herriman got into newspaper work as an artist, doing the requisite sports drawings and one-shot cartoons. He himself tried out a dozen of the different ideas for strips then current, and continuing to this day:

squabbling or anarchic families, funny obsessives, weird animals, aristocratic hoboes. William Randolph Hearst laughed so hard at one of his early strips that he sent a message to raise Herriman's salary on the spot. Eventually Herriman settled on the Dingbat family and their upstairs neighbors and their dog and cat—a cat who, quite incidentally in one 1912 strip, got bopped by a rock thrown by a mouse. Krazy Kat, if not exactly born, was "shadowed forth"—as Herriman might say.

Herriman's language was as great and as personal a creation as his drawing (which was true of Walt Kelly, too, and of no other strip artists). In the early strips, the fun of Herriman's language lay in its cheerful ransacking of the orotund and figure-laden language of American popular culture of the time, a style that all newspaper readers could be expected to recognize, one compounded of Victorian beauties, the circumlocutions of sensational crime reporting, stage melodrama, and even sermons. It continued in high-toned advertising and the titles used in silent movies ("Came the dawn . . . ") and it is a resource without which the work of humorists from Stephen Leacock through S. J. Perelman is unimaginable.

Joycean dream-echoes of this lost language can be heard throughout "Krazy Kat," further altered by being filtered through a dialect never spoken on land or sea, perhaps a compound of a Yiddish accent Herriman heard in New York mixed with a childhood memory of Creole—as vivid and personal a tongue, and as synthetic, as Kelly's swampdwellers would later speak. "In the dokk, dokk night an' the poily dawn," sings Krazy, "I'll be slippin' tight like a fency fawn—for I leff town a wikk iggo . . . on Tootsday."

The Sunday strips that Herriman did between 1916 and 1925 are the great surprise of this collection. Inventive, crowded with characters and settings and visual jokes and effects, exquisitely organized as whole pages, they are certainly one apex of Herriman's art. The other apex is the later, more scratchily drawn and leaner work, the daily permutations of mouse/cop/cat/brick/jail.

It would be possible, and a grotesque mistake, to conceive of Krazy Kat's endless tale (if it is a tale) as having something to do with the love/pain confusion of sadomasochism. When Krazy is hit with Ignatz' brick, hearts of love leap from his/her breast (Herriman never really decided Krazy's gender). When no brick comes, Krazy suffers loneliness. But this isn't perverse, it's something funnier than that, and more like life: It's a misunderstanding, pure and simple. Krazy Kat, pure of heart but not smart, is sure that Ignatz, whom she loves, loves her; the bricks are the proof. Ignatz, realist, no dope, wants only to drive home how little he loves Krazy, and is unable to grasp the pragmatical error he is making.

Officer Pup can't see that Krazy is not hurt by Ignatz' bricks; he is only shocked by Ignatz' cruelty to an innocent Kat. And Krazy is unable to perceive the drama between Ignatz and Pup, believing to the end that the arresting and jailing is a game they play for fun. An eternal twist of mutually exclusive universes—except when, in a blessed panel now and then, the three rest together, in the desert night, musing, freed for a moment from their compulsions.

The creator of these three characters would not himself have been capable of such compulsive behavior. He was a generous and sweet-natured man who loved animals and his friends and the Southwest and the gentle Navajos. (I was astonished to learn that Herriman's Coconino County is not imaginary, like Kelly's Pogofenokee, but a real place, in Arizona.) All who knew him agree; Herriman was some kind of saint, and more like fey, loving Krazy than tough Ignatz.

It occurs to me that, the proof sheets of nearly 30 years of "Krazy Kat" being extant, a newspaper might do itself and the public a great favor and just start printing them at the rate of one a day, as they were meant to be seen. The only argument against this that I can imagine is how the witless and brutal stuff beside them on today's unfunny pages would be hopelessly shamed by the strong and delicate art of George Herriman. So until some great paper takes the hint, well, you must buy this beautiful and well-made book, and read it slowly, one page a day—that's all.

1986?

WINSOR McCAY: HIS LIFE AND ART,
BY JOHN CANEMAKER

If George Herriman can be thought of as the Charlie Chaplin of the comic strip, then Winsor McCay is the Buster Keaton. Where Herriman's art was fey, off-center, touching and often profound, McCay's art was intellectual, plotted in long sequences of visual effects, almost geometric in its humor. In his greatest work, the big color pages of "Little Nemo in Slumberland," McCay is a master of euphoric movement, cool in his impact and almost serene even when he is attempting the horrific or the shocking, which isn't often. Little Nemo, perpetually surprised, innocent, easily spooked, and graceful in spite of himself—thanks to the acrobatic motions of the dream world around him—is a very Keatonesque character.

The movie comparison is apt. Not only was Winsor McCay fascinated by the graphic representation of motion and transformation, he was himself an early pioneer of film, and drew some early animated films. Unlike other animation artists, he drew every picture separately—400 drawings for one four-minute film. McCay had an astonishing quickness and huge capacity for work; he seems to have rarely stopped drawing his whole life long.

McCay and his time were in some ways ideally suited. The years of his greatest productivity coincided with the most vigorous years of the popular press in America, when New York had a dozen daily newspapers and William Randolph Hearst could start a war with Spain by his manipulations of public opinion. McCay did not start out a Hearst man, but he became one: Hearst bought his journalistic stars only after they had made huge names for themselves elsewhere, as McCay did at the New York Herald.

The richest and most informative parts of John Canemaker's biographical study for Abbeville Press are the early, pre-New York McCay pictures he provides in profusion, which show the varied ground out of which McCay's art grew: the circus posters and political cartoons, the city views (of Cincinnati, where his early work was done) and the constant practice in every kind of art jobbing. None of this would be lost when McCay came into his own.

And yet, despite the brilliance of his drawing, the strips that won McCay popularity ("Little Sammy Sneeze," "Dreams of a Rarebit Fiend") are only occasionally really compelling. McCay was hampered by a sense of humor utterly conventional and unsurprising. His jokes about wives' spending and henpecked husbands, Jersey mosquitoes, sneezing babies, are only redeemed by the irreal lengths to which he takes them—as when the wife's new hat grows to bandstand size and has to be brought home by teams of moving men.

But then there is "Little Nemo in Slumberland." The new strip did not arise without precedent, as *Alice in Wonderland* did, straight out of dream and onto the page, yet it is unlike anything McCay had done before. It made him rich and famous, and he continued it for years; it came to contain much lifeless prettiness and a large element of the pageant. But for a year or two, Winsor McCay was building a dream empire that really rivals the Alice books.

Night after night, little Nemo (whose name is Nobody, of course, as Odysseus's was once) sets out on a new dream journey toward Slumberland. Each night a psychopomp appears to guide him there, sent by the immense but kindly King of Slumberland, who wants to join Nemo with his Nemo-sized daughter. Each night the journey is frustrated; Nemo meets obstacles, or trips himself up, or breaks some dreamland prohibition; the creatures sent to help him desert or hinder him. Lost, in trouble, usually falling vertiginously, Nemo wakes up.

This narrative is fully (and, I suspect, wholly unconsciously) in the tradition of ancient and medieval dream romances, and at the same time wholly convincing as everyday (or everynight) dream-wanderings. It's made even more powerful when McCay introduces an odd little character named Flip: "an outcast member of the Dawn family, arch-enemies of Slumberland and its people." Canemaker has traced this figure to a cigar-smoking newsboy in Cincinnati and an aged black man McCay glimpsed in Brooklyn; he doesn't mention how much Flip combines the standard features of both vaudeville blackface comedians and stage Irishmen, the two "outcast" groups of McCay's own day.

Winsor McCay: His Life and Art *by John Canemaker*

Flip wears a hat with the words "Wake Up" written on it, and obviously stands for all that keeps Nemo from fulfillment in Slumberland. Intentionally or mischievously or brutally, Flip continually destroys the dream just as it is on the point of flowering.

That Flip, with his Irish/black/clown face, penile cigar, street talk, and naysaying, is the part of delicate bourgeois Nemo that Nemo must integrate to achieve Slumberland—not to wake up, but to make dreams fulfill themselves—is so startlingly obvious that it seems McCay must have intended it. That he didn't, that he wasn't secretly reading Jung, is proved by the fact that these marvelous tropes actually come to nothing. Slumberland is soon reached by both of them without the transformation that true romance would have required of the questing hero, and then left behind for other adventures.

So the instinctive grasp that McCay for a moment (a year or so) had of the matter and business of dreaming, loosened. What followed was often extraordinary and beautiful: the Moon, a lighter-than-air Mars, the Beaux-Arts palaces of Slumberland, visual transformations and effects unequalled in comic art. But the story—and the story is the other half of the comic strip—doesn't fulfill its early promise.

John Canemaker's biography is thorough and impressively illustrated, though often misguided about McCay's art, and burdened with a valiseful of psychobiographical cliches.

1987

TINTIN IN THE NEW WORLD
BY FREDERIC TUTEN

*T*HE LITERARY APOTHEOSIS of our pop-culture icons continues. Recently Geoff Ryman novelized Dorothy and Toto; Jay Cantor has made post-modernist hay out of the eternal triangulations of Krazy Kat. Now Frederic Tuten, an American novelist who lives much in France, has turned his gaze on Tintin, the eternal boy detective of French comics, or *bandes dessinées* as they say there.

Tintin first appeared in 1929, a creation of the Belgian artist George Remi, who used the name Hergé. Tintin went on fighting crime, accompanied by his faithful if usually drunken companion Captain Haddock, an old sea dog, and Snowy, a dog, for decades after, never growing older, in an indeterminate past time that (though it came to include space travel and international jets) was perhaps the author's childhood.

In Tuten's tale, Tintin, retired now from his detective adventuring, resides at a superb island mansion with his old companions, writing his memoirs. But though years have apparently passed, Tintin, a true cartoon icon, has remained twelve years old.

Of course his retirement is interrupted in the first pages. A message from Belgium (from his creator?) sends him forth again: "*Mon cher Tintin*, for some time now, our destinies have been linked, yours and mine... Always you have been sincere and intrepid. Were you the child of my own blood and not the personage of my dreams, I could wish no better." This time his adventure is to take him to Machu Picchu.

What he finds in the old hotel in the Peruvian Andes are not the traces of a criminal conspiracy but a quartet of characters from another mountain, the Magic Mountain of Thomas Mann's novel, written a few years before Tintin was created. Here are Settembrini the rational optimist, still arguing for democracy and progress, and Naptha the pessimistic authoritrarian, still contemptuous of free will; here is Peeperkorn, the mysterious Dutch epicurean, who has survived his suicide in Mann's book. And here is Clavdia Chauchat, Peeperkorn's companion, the enchantress who stirred the pot in the older novel, and under whose spell Tintin, the boy indifferent to grownup love, immediately falls.

Representing the New World among them is a chivalrous and sensitive Peruvian soldier, Lieutenant Nelson Dos Amantes, whose mind and heart are full of the plight of his land and people, the abused land and suppressed Indian peoples of the continent. He knows of the ancient messianic legends shared by many of them, and recognizes in Tintin's arrival a sign.

A good deal of what follows is not adventure but conversation, or debate, conducted in a peculiarly ornate rhetoric that sometimes reads as though translated from another language—indeed it sometimes echoes the stiff British English into which the original strips were translated. But it has other ambitions than moving the plot forward, and would fill many dozen panels with its extravagance:

"Perhaps I should puff a stout English pipe [Tintin proclaims], blow pensive rings at hearth's fender, and swirl my brandy till idle, indolent slumber takes me. Keep myself at home, I mean, among my books and toys, with the tight captain and the dog, companions of my ignorant youth and comrades of my premature dotage, for dotage it is to live without desire or without wishing to inform each hour with personal intent."

There is lots more like this, from all parties. The reader begins to believe he has found himself in that wearying thing, a philosophical romance; and what is worse, suspects that little or none of the debates about the nature of crime, the proper governance of society, the fate of mankind, freedom and hope vs. control and despair, are quite serious.

But slowly the book, like Tintin, begins to grow. Tintin, who has lost his virginity though not his innocence with Clavdia, is taken up by Peeperkorn, who insists on describing to him the grownup world of rapacious love, and eternal self-love, which Clavdia inhabits. He tells a long story about his own fall from riches and his climb back up again. He begins to show himself as one of the necessary characters of picaresque, the unkillable tormentor and guide capable of endless self-transformation, who bears a secret about the hero.

Who, he wants to know, are Tintin's parents? His father disappeared before Tintin knew him; have not Tintin's repetitious adventures been a disguised revenge on his father for his abandonment, a means of proving his worth to his mother? The lineaments of a different kind of romance are shadowed forth, psychoanalytic, even Oedipal.

But the book outgrows this mode too, as it outgrew the barren literary teasing, and just in time. Tintin has more growing to do, and the book expands with him, and while hovering always on a precipice of absurdity (as it has hovered at the precipice of Machu Picchu for many chapters) rises at length to a grave and moving myth-making. The world turns, and becomes new; Tintin is forever.

This is a book that would doubtless repay re-reading; its secrets are laid deep, beneath a deceptively lucid surface. An astute reader (more astute and erudite than the present reviewer) will perhaps be able to guess the sources of the many paragraphs in quotations embedded in the text. Just Tuten? Or another Mann?

1993

THE WORLD OF EDWARD GOREY BY
CLIFFORD ROSS AND KAREN WILKIN

*I*N 1962, LOOKING IN some bewilderment for a Christmas present for my college-age sister, I picked up a pretty little "gift book" in a stationery store: *The Willowdale Handcar* by (as every literate person now knows and almost nobody knew then) Edward Gorey. In it, three young people in a turn-of-the-century rural America take a handcar on a whim, travel through a sensational and drastic plot without understanding it, and never return. It was the right size and the right price, and I thought she'd like the funny old-fashioned drawings. I didn't understand, though I soon would and my sister too, that here was a small masterpiece. I still regard it as among the author's very best: a curt yet extravagant anti-story that mixed parody (but of what exactly?) with nameless dread and deadpan silliness: "Between West Elbow and Penetralia, they almost ran over someone who was tied to the tracks. It proved to be Nellie."

We had made a discovery. Next year she gave me *The Fatal Lozenge* (too weird) and we found *The Vinegar Works* (too ghastly) and then *The Doubtful Guest*, which was, like *The Willowdale Handcar*, an exquisite mix of the absurd and the sinister, instantly pleasing. But I kept studying the odd ones: *The West Wing* (no text, only the empty rooms and desolation) and *The Object-lesson* ("... the tea-urn empty, save for a card on which was written a single word: Farewell.") They could not, it seemed, be used up.

To discover others who knew Gorey was rare then, and wonderful; when I first moved to New York I met a fellow-enthusiast who claimed that Gorey lived right nearby, in Murray Hill—and there he was, in the phone book! Should we call him? We did, but my confederate, on hearing an actual human hello, hung up in confusion without speaking. How did Gorey respond? We imagined him returning to a vast armchair, peeling a bit of rubber from the sole of a white canvas shoe, and perhaps laying out the old fantod deck in search of answers.

Now, of course, Gorey belongs to us all; we might reflect on how much the small self-selected readership, the little books sold only in the better shops and passed on from initiate to novice, was part of the overall effect of his work, but all that has vanished as he has become known for his Broadway stage designs, big anthologies, television titles and the usual panoply of notecards, toys, games and coffee-mugs. The present album is a culmination of a kind, a fond and flattering panegyric delivered to one who is now (how surprised we would have been in 1962 to know it) an "icon."

The World of Edward Gorey contains plates previously published and unpublished from every phase of Gorey's career, beautifully reproduced; working drawings and sketches; theater programs and posters, set designs, and book jackets; an interview with Gorey conducted by Clifford Ross ("I have lots of iron utensils. I buy those quite cheap at yard sales. I have trunks full of that stuff") and an appreciation by Karen Wilkins that is unexceptionable ("On the surface, it is all very gloomy, yet none of the apparent horrors really seem to matter," she says, quite justly). Of course we want to have all this, and the photographs of Gorey's book-crammed workspaces in Cape Cod, and the handy chronology ("1957: Begins attending performances of the New York City Ballet. Maintains perfect record of attendance until 1982.") Our knowledge of Gorey is not exactly expanded, however, for little that we learn is unexpected: in fact, the *thinness* of Gorey's work—I don't use the word pejoratively—is made the more apparent, and the more perilous.

Wilkins remarks in her essay on the brief Gorey cast of characters, nearly complete from the beginning; notes the flatness and simplicity of the frame he generally uses—his pictures remind me of the little box sets, shot full on, that were a feature of early silent movies: rooms the characters entered and left, as the titles told the story. (Early silents are one of the few influences on Gorey that Wilkins doesn't mention.) The marvelous effect of his work is due to the strict abnegation of his means: how within the set limits he can suggest poignancy, wonder, hope and other large feelings, and not only entrapment and artifice.

The danger is that the oftener the trick is repeated the less likely it is to come off, for it depends on surprise—we didn't think we could be touched in this funny thin world, and yet we are. *En masse* the thinness can seem merely thin; self-parody (something only the original and distinctive artist is liable to) threatens. The dread his early work was soaked in becomes finally a gesture, just kidding, and makes it seem to have been just kidding all along. We remain charmed, but may, finally, cease to be moved.

No matter. Gorey is the author of the best book ever written about the process of writing a novel (*The Unstrung Harp; or, Mr. Earbrass Writes a Novel*, his first) and a body of unwritten but still somehow existent novels (e.g., *The Secrets, Volume One: The Other Statue*, 1968) that fill a precious bookshelf in the imagination. All Goreyans will want this nicely-produced tribute, and deserve to have it in their stockings.

1996

~ WALT KELLEY ~

I HAVE SPENT THE LAST months reading through many of the collected daily strips of Walt Kelly's *Pogo* from 1948 to 1960. It was—among other things—an excursus in the unreliability of memory. Often I found I had misremembered panels and stories that I believed had been fixed exactly and forever in my memory on the day they first appeared, or at least by my passionate and constant re-reading starting on the day after every Christmas, when I would devour a year's worth of strips in anthology form, before studying every page more exhaustively. I was certain, for instance, that it was the three bats (Bewitched, Bothered and Bemildred) who are seen poling down the river in a wooden soda crate on which is written "Pensacola—It's the Spa." It's not; it's the two Cowbirds. I don't remember that it was the Crane, Roogey Batoon, who remarked (on Snavely the Snake's rejecting him), "How sharper than a child's tooth, a Serpent's ingratitude." I remember Snavely himself saying it, concerning the Worm Chile who is in training to be a snake, and more wittily curtailed too: "Ingratitude—How sharper than a Child's tooth, etc." Kelly does repeat a few jokes, and maybe I lighted on these instances and not the ones I recall. On the other hand, I remembered almost every panel I looked at, many of which I had not seen in fifty years, though they seemed different—maybe because I understand them now differently. After all, this is an immense *ouevre*, even if the fading last years are excluded from consideration (as I have excluded them in this study, unable to bring myself to examine them, remembering the sadness they evoked in me even as a young adult).

I didn't at age eleven know that the "serpent's tooth" quote came from *King Lear*—it's possible Kelley didn't either. It was simply part of the generally known mass of literary and Biblical tags, Victorian pop culture, and sentimental music references that everyone growing up when Kelley did could recognize. "Pail Hans I love, beside the Tugaloo," sings Churchy LaFemme the turtle, and Kelley could count on his readers hearing with an inward ear the old song "Pale hands I loved, beside the Shalimar." Churchy's name, of course (for no obvious reason) is taken from the phrase that Dumas supposedly coined as the secret to solving a mystery, *Cherchez la femme*.

But let's—for the sake of younger readers, the unamused, those unfamiliar with the work, and those who have forgotten it and don't regret it—start at the beginning.

Walt Kelly always thought of himself as a newspaperman, and his early career in journalism in his hometown of Bridgeport, Connecticut, involved him in all the varied trades of drawing for reproduction as well, including political cartooning. In the 1930s he went out to Hollywood to work in the Disney stable, but after the 1941 strike at the studio he fled back to weary and beclouded New England where he belonged—his characters and their behavior, language, obsessions and referents are all derived from the world of Bridgeport and New York (and not, of course, from the South at all, about which he knew nothing). From Disney he learned very little (the three-fingered hand, maybe, and the way in which a cartoon animal may wear its shirt and not pants, and yet feel embarrassed to remove it in public or before the Opposite Sex). It is interesting though that Pogo, physically and characterologically, undergoes a transformation somewhat like Mickey's—from a long-nosed, small-eyed, somewhat rascally and amoral scamp to a short-nosed, big-headed, wide-eyed and smiling innocent. Stephen Jay Gould once pointed out how this physical transformation, a kind of reverse maturing, makes Mickey increasingly resemble an infant, and thus more lovable.

Supporting himself with endless jobbery, Kelly now turned out a number of comic books, and one series he did for *Animal Comics* featured a Southland cast headed by a possum and an alligator, as well as a human black child called Bumbazine. After service in the Army during World War II, Kelly joined the staff of a new New York daily paper called the *Star*, and it was there that *Pogo* (minus the human child, whose presence somehow inhibited the animals from being human themselves) first appeared as a daily strip. When the quixotic liberal *Star* folded, Kelly got a farseeing syndicator to take on *Pogo*. (I have all this history from the volumes of the complete daily strips now coming out from Fantagraphics Books, introduced with great thoroughness by R.C. Harvey.) The later Kelly/*Pogo* work includes not only the daily and a Sunday strip, but further comic books with the new cast, and a number of paperbacks containing fractured fairy tales and parodies enacted by the *Pogo* regulars. Some of these are brilliant and wildly peculiar, but in what follows I discuss only the daily strips. I read them from 1949 to 1951 in the Brattleboro (VT) *Reformer*, and after I left for a Pogoless hinterland, in the yearly anthologies, which came with extra songs.

Ever since French intellectuals took up the *bande desinée* with the same enthusiasm they had American gangster and cowboy films, the art of the comic strip has gained in cultural status. In the 1960s, like many popular forms from surfing music to pornography, it was taken up by artists who were self-conscious and also conscious of the history of their art; the recent "graphic novelists" such as Ben Katchor and Art Spielgelman are treated today with the reverence granted to any artist we feel is in control of both material and impulse. No history of the American comic strip, or the comic book either, could exclude Kelly and *Pogo*, though they stand at the moment on rather shaky critical footing. George Herriman (*Krazy Kat*) and Winsor Mackay (*Little Nemo in Slumberland*) are undisputed early masters, and the contenders for the bronze are many; far greater are the numbers of the much-beloved and the fondly-remembered. Despite the critical attention, standards tend to the subjective, and derive in part from childhood (for those old enough to have seen these works as they appeared). I despised *Li'l Abner* (though I read it constantly) and was left cold by *Dondi* and *Prince Valiant*. When in the course of a review of Ben Katchor's work I claimed for *Pogo* a place in the first rank, my editor (J.D. McClatchy) demurred, though he let it pass.

The art of the comic strip is a mixed one, combining words and pictures in what ought to be an equality of creativity. Narrative is a common feature, but only an option; there are many comic strips that never progress in time at all, but merely run variations on an eternal unchanging situation (*Peanuts* and *Krazy Kat*) and only a few extend the idea of narrative so far as to have characters age over time (*Joe Palooka, Gasoline Alley*). *Pogo* was one that told continuous stories, some of them months long, most of them unresolved finally or metamorphosing into others; new stories tended to begin either with the introduction of a new character or an older character's sudden adoption of a new idea, often a get-rich-quick scheme or a sudden burst of paranoia, as when Albert the Alligator grows alarmed at the world's plans to populate the moon and sets out to defend it, or Howland Owl conceives it the duty of the Swamp to develop its own atomic weapons ("These here nuclear physics is neither new nor clear"). Comic strips such as *Pogo* proceed, as movies do, by action and words combined, and which has the dominant role can change. Kelly was a master of visual slapstick, but his complex frames of action are made much funnier by the unique baroque tongue-twisting language at which Kelly excelled; in many stories, panel after panel can go by with characters at rest, heads on a comfortable log, talking and talking, with only their mobile features and the expansive and expressive lettering in action.

There is far more talk in *Pogo* than in any modern strip. Outside of Dickens, I can't think of a crowd of characters made so distinct by the language they use. Beauregard the bloodhound is given to highflown self-regarding sentiments. Seminole Sam the salesman fox is not Southern at all but a Yankee con man and publicist with a great line of adman gas: "We're standing with our feet buttered on a pool of ball bearings," he notes, as he plans Pogo's perennial Presidential campaign. "The *TRUTH* is TRICKY... One man's truth is another man's COLD BROCCOLI... Our job, Chief, is to make the truth *TASTY*." To which Howland Owl (who tends to adopt whatever discourse he's next to) replies, "You're *RIGHT!* Rummagin' thru the ice box for STALE STERLING don't cut NO notches on the WATER PISTOL."

The circus-poster speech-balloons of impresario P.T. Bridgeport, the black-bordered funeral cards of buzzard Sarcophagus MacAbre's, Deacon Mushrat's Olde English, define character instantly by themselves; what's more interesting to me is the unitary effect of the Kelly language, which though it has a variety of modes, is consistent throughout. Of course the language has nothing to do with any "southern" speech ever heard anywhere. Though some of what might be called "stage Southern", on the model of "stage Irish", creep in, the "ever-lovin' blue-eyed dag-blagged lil' scapers" sort of thing, the whole is unrelated even to American illiterate speech in general. It has less in common with Joel Chandler Harris or other rural wits than it has with the synthetic language of Herriman's *Krazy Kat* and, arguably, the Irish of James Joyce. The constancy of puns and wordplay; the subtle transmogrification of words into unrelated but significant other words that shadow them; the misheard, misremembered, and mis-spoken—the language not only drives the strips forward, it embellishes the corners and backgrounds of panel upon panel with play that is not quite nonsense: *Sent under separate cover of darkness . . . Support you in the style to which you are a customer . . . Romeo wasn't bilked in a day . . . It don't pay to Tinker for Ever with Chance . . . To corn a phrase . . . Another day another dullard . . . Girl of the Limberwurst . . . Never dark on the door again.*

Though the cast of *Pogo* is never seen leaving the environs of the swamp—they are never even seen in the semi-mythical town of Fort Mudge, often spoken of as the nearby urban center whence the train or trolley departs for the world—many of the characters come to the swamp from elsewhere; the comedy and poetry of American place names, not always rendered correctly, were dear to Kelly, and I suspect were part of the patter of journeyman con-artists, tall-tale-tellers, and jacks-of-all-trades in the vagrant Depression years, when men went far for work or to relieve their families of their upkeep; this may be my own sentimental image. "You is the spit and image of Grandpa Puddlewheel—the biggest boat-tailed Grackle west of Fargo and north of Fort Mudge . . . " "As Maine goes, oh so goes Oswego . . . " "a view of Altoona in 1908 for you to admire . . . " "Paddlin' all the way home from JERSEY CITY on a blowed-up rubber horse . . . " "The best-dressed men south of Winnepegosis . . . " Etc.

I can't argue that the elaborate and continuous verbal play is really distinctly Irish, or even Irish-American, though it was a constant feature of my own household, and seems to me clearly related not only to innate (or at least highly regarded and rewarded) verbal facility, but also to a compulsion to put signifiers in doubt, where the signified (sex, say, or money, or religion) is hard to approach directly, if at all. Hilarity then substitutes for perspicuity, as on almost every *Pogo* page. It's a tribute to Kelly's *pictorial* art that some of the loveliest exchanges don't translate well onto the page denuded both of their calligraphy and the characters' expressions.

I'll try one and you'll see. Churchy, Mouse and Bun Rab the obsessive drummer boy are getting ready to practice carols:

> CHURCHY: Now, if we clear our throats with ASCAP, we'll be all set.
> MOUSE (*Checks sheet music)*: HOLD IT! "Silent Night" is effective played *FORTISSIMO* on a steam calliope.
> CHURCHY: Our steam calliope was traded to CLEVELAND for a second baseman an' a pitchpipe.
> MOUSE: Then I'll carry the tenor (providin' he has a light rein).
> BUN RAB: Here's the KEY ... (*Plays:)* BLOO **BLOO**
> CHURCHY: BLOO? What kind of a key is THAT?
> BUN RAB: Bloo? Old Bloo is a YALE KEY ... Want to make something of it?
> MOUSE: Yes ... We could make lovely bolt for the door.

Not only does this lie rather flatly on the page, where its inventiveness seems a little operose, it is bound to annoy those who mistrust or see no fun in puns or purely verbal humor, or worse, suspect the punner of mockery or otherwise scheming for advantage. What interested me when I first encountered it, though I only became conscious of it later, is the way in which this verbal byplay, though sometimes brought out by rage or confusion, is just as often deliberate on a character's part—you can see it in the self-satisfied smile and upcast eyes of the Mouse on that last line about making a bolt for the door, and a similar expression can be seen on others' faces.

In most modern strips—and I don't know if it's because the work seems too hard to modern draughtspeople, or because blank-faced affectlessness is the mode, or the knack is lost—the characters have little variety in emotional expression. *Dilbert* and *Doonesbury* are witty and poignant, but the faces are relatively unchanging; in fact that's part of the humor. *Pogo* people express a range of emotions as clearly as silent-movie actors, from steely resolve to mind-blown amazement to indignant rage to subtle shame to abashed confusion. Kelly's pen is marvelously swift in the capturing of expression, and fine effects are achieved by a clash between words and face; transfigured storytellers are nicely capture but so are the bored or doubtful listeners behind. Of course the elaborate yet fluid chiaroscuro of Kelly's black-and-white strips is itself largely a thing of the past—Robert Crumb in effect reinvented it for himself in the late 1960s, and the only recent daily newspaper strip that approached Kelly's emotional variety in the drawing is, or rather was, *Calvin and Hobbes*, which owed a great deal to the Kelly style, and still restricted itself to a small cast.

The mystery that *Pogo* presents, then, is how these miniature cartoon beings, not even people, not even animals for that matter, sketchily drawn however skillfully, can evoke in a reader such a range of feeling. Is there a bare minimum of representation that we can respond to as fully limning us? Do the bodies of our souls perhaps have these longways oval eyes, though our physical bodies don't, so that we can respond to them as the eyes (compelling, alive, full of character) of fellow creatures with inner lives as rich as our own?

A great and unlikely achievement of the strip, considered as a single *roman fleuve* or Balzacian multi-volume human comedy, is its surprising moral complexity, which in turn draws on a kind of deep darkness outside or beneath the sunny silliness. It's usual to note that Kelly was an interested, even a passionate, observer of the American political and social scene in the 1950s, and his work is filled with (some would say marred by) topical humor, comment, and satire. Kelly started as a political cartoonist, and in a sense remained one. (When *Mad* magazine parodied *Pogo* in the early Fifties, it had all the swampland critters turn into political figures—Howland Owl was "Marshland Tito" and Churchy became Pierre Mendes-France with his glass of milk.) The McCarthy phenomenon was chief among his preoccupations, and it ramified and spread in several directions through the Pogo world. In one way or another almost all the characters get involved in realms of suspicion, blame, threat, fear, and demands for conformity and orthodoxy. How each responds is unpredictable, and while never ceasing to be funny, and never succeeding in turning us against characters we favor and love, the responses of some are unsettling, and go far beyond the simplicities of political satire.

A set of decidedly unpleasant characters, unpleasant in different ways, were a feature of the strip from early on. There is Deacon Mushrat, deeply mendacious but weak, and hypocritical too, as befits his calling and the Olde English lettering in which he speaks;

Wiley Catt, backwoods lyncher; Mole MacCarony, intelligent, humorless and coldly cunning; and Simple J. Malarkey, a sort of more potent Wiley Catt, with the serpent-cold eyes and weird linguistic turns of Senator McCarthy himself. At first, the more villainous characters are occupied with catching and eating the smaller and weaker animals like Pogo and Churchy the turtle—in other words, they are standard animal-tale villains, like Br'er Bear. But in later tales the villainy is more diffuse and far-reaching; the villains become embroiled in their own plots, and the simpler characters can be swept up in rampant enthusiasms without really understanding the consequences.

An early instance is the 1950 story in which the Pup Dog is lost, and suspicion falls on Albert the Alligator, who in his role as the strip's Id, is suspected of having eaten him. The "unvestigators" are determined to arrest and try him. (Their authority is only their own assertion, but even the wiser characters like Pogo and Porky Pine accept it.) Howland Owl is willing to act as a hanging judge. Seminole Sam the fox is prosecuting attorney, and he suborns Churchy, an unsuspicious and innocent fellow most of the time, into raiding Albert's garbage can for evidence. He finds the skeleton that Sam thought he'd find, though it's a fish's ("*WITNESS*, was the poor l'il Pup Dog fond of the *WATER?*" Sam asks, introducing it into evidence. "He was just like a *FISH*, would you say, Witness?") The most touching moment of the episode comes, however, when Pogo and Porky Pine (the only characters whose hearts are always in the right place) try to convince Albert to hide in the swamp to avoid prosecution. "Where's yo' manners, chillun?" says Albert, firmly. "If a couple strangers wishes to interrOgate a Southern gentleman, *THEY GITS THEIR CHANCE*... I gone stroll over this way."

In March 1953 the Boy Bird Watchers, organized by Deacon Mushrat at first to keep track of the habits of birds (using the indispensable *Cap'n Wimby's Bird Atlas*) is taken over by Mole MacCarony and Simple J. Malarkey and expanded into a general vigilante committee. They alone will decide who is a bird (though the Mole is nearly blind, and can't see who is before him). Who will be brave, who will rise to the occasion, who will turn tail, who will act in self-serving and self-fooling ways, is never certain along the broad middle of the character spectrum. The amoral Bats are willing to serve any master; Deacon struggles to retain a shred of power and dignity. The Cowbirds, having been persecuted, are ready to persecute. Mole insists that, as an owl, Owl is required to migrate by the first of April ("You have a day to pack") and when Owl appeals to *Cap'n Wimby's*, Mole claims it's "discredited" and sets it on fire: "There's nothing quite so lovely as a brightly burning book," he says. Owl does his best to remember how to fly. This episode ends in the falling-out and murderous confrontation of Mole and Malarkey, a moment I found genuinely chilling in 1953 and still do.

In other episodes Howland Owl is never far from *trahison des clercs*, and indulgence in intellectual obsessions leads him into fantasies of power and scope (Howland's steely-eyed *gravitas* is a wonderful Kelly face). Churchy is a little too brainless to resist evil at first, though too good-natured to persist in it. Albert can be led astray by his ego and by flattery (including his own) and the Hound Dog can convince himself that his high self-esteem requires vigilance and action (of all the characters, he is most likely to be found having appointed himself to official positions, as game warden, policeman, or fireman). The hilarity that arises from the errors that all these characters make about what's going on—whether from avarice, self-delusion, or plain stupidity—have a certain extra edge when what is going on is witch-hunting, power-grabbing and ostracism of their fellows. I think I grasped this even as a child—there seemed to be, sometimes though rarely, more at stake in *Pogo* than in *Smoky Stover* or *The Little King* or *Henry*, though just what I wasn't always clear about.

The two Cowbirds, for instance, were a puzzle to me. Kelly, like all committed liberals, had to make it clear that he was not soft on Communism, or even pink himself, and he did so by including these characters, and putting them through some funny paces. Actual cowbirds, of course, lay their eggs in the nests of other birds, who are forced to raise the greedy and usually larger young as their own. The *Pogo* Cowbirds are Communists, probably Party members, though that's unclear—they certainly tend to follow the Moscow line, they credit Russians with inventing baseball and other things, and get occasional postcards in Russian ("How come you birds are gettin' postcards in Russian?" "How come you *knows* its Russian?") The two begin as fairly small birds, and at one point they do a Whitaker Chambers and turn coats, joining the Boy Bird

Watchers to expiate their former errors; later they have grown larger and more crowlike, are dressed in beatnik berets and turtlenecks, and debate Party policy and voice resentment at length. Kelly thus conflates the left with the Party and its Soviet masters in the same way that the right-wing paranoids he makes fun of also did. It was a different world.

But I have fallen into the commonplace error I decried only a few paragraphs past, of considering Kelly chiefly as a social satirist and commentator, which was the least becoming of his hats. (I also have to beware of attempting to imitate, or parody, the Kelly prose style, as almost every commentator on his work—not excepting himself—seems compelled to do.)

The actual continuing interest of the strip, and the preoccupation of its characters much of the time, is not political but ontological. *Pogo* people are continuously in doubt as to whether they are themselves or someone else; they can disguise themselves as one another, or as other personages (Lulu Arfin' Nanny, with the blunked-out eyeballs) and then forget whether they are themselves or the disguise. The three Bats named above are constantly forgetting which of them is which, a puzzle that interrupts their continual mad card game; the only clue is which of their three pairs of differently patterned pants they happen to have on. If a character knocks on another's door, is not admitted, then goes around through the window just as the character inside opens the door to find no one there, the first character is just as puzzled as the second as to who could have come calling. When Porky Pine's brutally amoral Uncle Baldwin enters the strip and insists that no one can determine he's not Porky, even Porky has to admit the force of his argument—he abandons his house to his uncle, and goes off alone to brood.

Though it's never certain which of the characters will be able to see through the disguises of which others, it seems to be a rough measure of level-headedness, temporary at least, to do so—characters like Porky Pine and Miz Rackety Coon are rarely fooled, and I think Pogo never is. The semiotics of personality, the persistence of self through time, the instability of identity and the equivalence of social role (changeable) with self-conception are endlessly upended, and Theory ought to revel in the epistemologies (amounting conceivably to bad faith, as the Cowbirds are always, in bad faith, insisting) run amok herein.

If Theory is to be invoked, though, it seems to me that the categories of Bakhtinian criticism are more useful. *Pogo* is as dialogic as a Dickens novel; there is no master narrator, and the voices are not only those of the characters but, as noted, of the whole talkative American culture of the period and the past, from political screeds to circus promotions, advertising jingles ("Chonko, the Nutty Chew"), newspapers and magazines ("*Newslife*, The Magazine of Togetherheid"), and other comics, all swirling together, detached from their sources and seething in the general perloo of thought and action—what Bakhtin calls *heteroglossia*. Take the time that Howland Owl convinces Albert to (once again) disguise himself as silent scream star Lulu Arfin' Nanny, Queen of the Dogs. Suddenly the language of sensational film rushes in as Albert not only disguises himself as but *becomes* a vamp ("Keez me, you fool!"). Informed by Owl that Lulu was not a sireen but a homebody, Albert takes the cue, and swings Owl in a Charleston:

"A little homebody
An' a little home brew
In a little posy rosy covered BUNG-aloo!
Built for BABY MINE and your SHEIK makes two —
With PUDDLES of SUNSHINE,
And MILLIONS OF BLISS,
Hug me, honey bunny, with a GOOD NIGHT KISS . . .
'Cause I'm a GOOD-BYE, GOOD-BYE, GOOD-BYE Miss!"

When he complacently asks Owl "What early movie queen does I remind you of?", Owl replies, "The late Gertie the Dinosaur." But they join up at the piano for a second chorus, with Owl on violin:

"A little homebody
An' a little home brew
Crazin' to amazin' Dixie line or two,
Shovel an' shuffle in your shifty shoe —
Da da! Da da! Da da! Da DUM!
My little home biddy's bitty eye of blue
With a dinky, pinky, winky, quickie blue boo hoo,
SNIFFLE an' SNUFFLE but it's TOODLE-OO
Tibby—tubby—tabby . . . . TA-BOO!"

This last word comes as Owl busses an astonished Albert in the famous pose of the Tabu perfume ads, wherein a violinist embraces a pianist swept away by the music. Try singing it—the tune will come automatically.

"Carnivalesque" is another of Bakhtin's key terms. Laughter dissolves the past; in the comic world there is "nothing for memory and tradition to do." The laughter generated by the carnivalesque work "demolishes fear and piety before an object;" laughter is a "preresuisite for fearlessness, without which it would be impossible to approach the world realistically." *Pogo* taken as a single work (the daily strips, that is) is what Bakhtin called a "laughing novel," with its fools playing at being wisemen, authority upended, identities continually unsettled and swapped, pieties translated into nonsense, and all serious conflicts resolved in eating, drinking and singing. All that is missing from the equation is human physicality: Rabelaisian farting, swiving and excreting are transcended by the talking-animal fantasy bodies.

But, while acknowledging these large interpretations, I think there is an easier way to account for what goes on in most of *Pogo*, though it didn't occur to me until I had grown up and had children, and watched them grow: above all, it seems to me, what goes on in the Swamp is very like what goes on in many a backyard. The interplay of imagination and asserted reality, whereby the same small cast continually reinvents itself by donning old clothes, and asserts the new roles (with their concomitant power and responsibility) until weariness sets in or a fight breaks out; the ability to travel great distances and go on long adventures within a very small space; the cheerful forgetting of rages and obsessions as soon as new amusements arise; even the inchoate language and the moral ambiguities seem a part of child-life. What clued me in was the legs and feet: studying these fat little legs and bare toes, I suddenly realized I was looking at children (probably Kelly's own), and this made a new sense out of the constant inventiveness and play—the space ships and mechanical men made of junk, the teevee station made of an old bureau with empty mirror frame. The paralyzing shyness of the male characters in the face of sexuality fits with this conception as well—they all court Miz Hepzibah the Parisian skunk, though they never get farther than delivering the flowers (or pail of fish) before being overcome with nerves and running away, unless food is on offer. So it used to be with little boys and little girls, some of the time anyway, and though it's different now, it's not all different.

In a famous essay about Dickens called *Dingley Dell and the Fleet*, W.H. Auden made a useful distinction (distinctions between opposed things was Auden's mode of thought). "Our dream pictures of the Happy Place where suffering and evil are unknown are of two kinds, the Edens and the New Jerusalems," he says, and between the dreamer of Eden (or Arcadia) and the planner of Utopia the "gulf is unbridgeable." Pogofenokee is surely not a New Jerusalem, where everyone wants to do what they should do; on the other hand, Auden's descriptive axioms of Eden (where you ought to do whatever you want) mostly apply. "Eden is a world of pure being and absolute uniqueness... Everyone is incomparable." Certainly this is the *Pogo* case, especially since all the animals are different species; when a second animal of a given species appears, it usually starts an agon about identity. "There is no distinction between the objective and the subjective. What a person appears to be is identical to what he is to himself. His name and his clothes are as much *his* as his body, so that, if he changes them, he turns into someone else." This is, as stated above, central to the Pogo world.

"Space is both safe and free," Auden's list continues. "There are walled gardens but no dungeons." In *Pogo* almost everyone immured is immured by error, and all are eventually freed. "Whatever people do, whether alone or in company, is some kind of play... no deed has a goal or an effect beyond itself." As children abandon any seriously-meant activity as soon as it runs out of steam, so do the *Pogo* characters (and their author), usually in a festive gathering that includes the putatively wicked, or the irruption of a holiday that needs to be celebrated. "Three kinds of erotic life are possible, though any particular dream of Eden need contain only one"—the three being polymorphous guiltless (and shameless) promiscuity, courting that never issues in marriage, and "the chastity of natural celibates without desire." The (male) characters in *Pogo* are all described by the latter two, usually by both at once—not for them the randy random sexuality of early cartoons, for instance, with their sexy cows and horny cats.

"The Serpent, acquaintance with whom results in immediate expulsion—any serious need or desire." Any serious fear or grief as well, I think, the ever-present possibility of which is, in *Pogo*, always mitigated by the language, whose lability divorces sense from responsibility, though not, I would claim, from seriousness. As Nietzsche says, "To become mature is to recover that sense of seriousness which one had as a child at play." The activities of the *Pogo* characters are, like those of children, free from seriousness as we observe them, but not as they are experienced by the characters themselves: if it were not so, they would be trivial. The dark menace that, as I have noted, sometimes intrudes amid them, and sorts them into the few who are brave and wise and the many who are less so, proceeds into their Eden from the outside (adult) world, which they can consider and imitate but not in the end be truly harmed by. And isn't this what we would wish for children too: that their space be both safe and free? Yet we know the menace to be there.

The Utopian, Auden points out, looks always forward. His griefs are irritation and rage at incompletion. The dreamer of Eden looks backward to a world complete but impossible to return to, and the causes of his expulsion are no part of his dream; his trouble is melancholy. (Think how many imagined Edens need a single melancholic to stand apart from and set off the fun, like Jacques in *As You Like It*, or Porky Pine in *Pogo*.) The expulsion from childhood is a related experience, even though few childhoods are really Edenic in retrospect—the understanding that nothing is or was ever really Edenic is part of the loss of Eden. *Pogo* is dream-Edenic, a world at once ever-novel and changeless (it thinned and vanished eventually, for though there was no death in that Arcadia, Kelly was mortal), and it resembles the Edenic world of childhood in its salvific aspects—insofar as I am fearless, and approach the world realistically, I am so in part because of the laughing novel *Pogo*. I loved it unreservedly as a child, and it is bound up with my own childhood: so my necessary expulsion from the one Eden only increases my longtime delight in the other, and also the melancholy at the heart of my contemplation. And yet, again:

"A song not for Now
You need not put stay . . .
A tune for the Was
Can be sung for Today . . .
The notes of the Does-not

*Will sound as the Does . . .
Today you can sing
For the Will-be that was."*

2004/2005